KETO DIET

A SIMPLE AND EFFECTIVE GUIDE TO LOSING WEIGHT FOR BEGINNERS

Jacob Greene

Tiffany Greene

© Copyright 2019 - All rights reserved.

The contents of this book may not be reproduced, duplicated or transmitted without direct written permission from the author.

Under no circumstances will any legal responsibility or blame be held against the publisher for any reparation, damages, or monetary loss due to the information herein, either directly or indirectly.

Legal Notice:

You cannot amend, distribute, sell, use, quote or paraphrase any part of the content within this book without the consent of the author.

Disclaimer Notice:

Please note the information contained within this document is for educational and entertainment purposes only. No warranties of any kind are expressed or implied. Readers acknowledge that the author is not engaging in the rendering of legal, financial, medical or professional advice. Please consult a licensed professional before attempting any techniques outlined in this book.

By reading this document, the reader agrees that under no circumstances are the author responsible for any losses, direct or indirect, which are incurred as a result of the use of information contained within this document, including, but not limited to, —errors, omissions, or inaccuracies.

Table of Contents

INTRODUCTION IX
CHAPTER ONE THE KETOGENIC DIET AND ITS BENEFITS 1
CHAPTER TWO KETOGENIC FOODS TO EAT AND AVOID 7
CHAPTER THREE SEVEN WAYS TO GET INTO KETOSIS 11
CHAPTER FOUR DEBUNKING KETOGENIC DIET MYTHS 16
CHAPTER FIVE KETO TIPS FOR BEGINNERS 21
CHAPTER SIX KETO BREAKFAST RECIPES 27
    Avocado Breakfast Bowl 28
    Chorizo Shakshuka 29
    Keto Mexican Scrambled eggs 32
    Keto fried eggs with kale and pork 33
    Cauliflower and Kale Frittata in an Instant pot 35
    Keto seafood omelette 36
    Keto egg muffins 37
    Strawberry Chocolate crepes 38
    Instant pot Cauliflower Hash Brown Casserole 39
    Lemon and blueberry muffins 40
    Rosemary Bagels 42
    Instant Pot Melamen 43
CHAPTER SEVEN KETO SOUP RECIPES **44**
    Hot and Sour Vegetable Soup 46
    Chicken Mushroom Soup in an Instant Pot 48
    Creamy Spinach Soup 49
    Chicken Soup 50
    Instant Pot Low Carb Taco Soup 51
    Thai Coconut Soup 53
    Chicken and Bacon Soup 55
    Thai Curry Soup with Tofu 57
    Roasted Tomato Soup 58
    Chicken Fajita Soup 59
    High Fat Hamburger Soup 60
CHAPTER EIGHT KETO SMOOTHIE RECIPES **62**

- Avocado and Coconut water Smoothie 64
- Butter Smoothie 65
- Spicy Green Smoothie 67
- Strawberry Hemp Seed Smoothie 68
- Strawberry Rhubarb Smoothie 69
- Green Devil 70
- Pumpkin Spice Latte Smoothie 71
- Very Berry Smoothie 72
- Vegetable Smoothie 73
- McKeto Strawberry Milkshake 74
- Spicy Tomato Smoothie 75
- Strawberries 'n' Cream Smoothie Bowl 76
- Egg Cream Smoothie 77
- Salted Caramel Cashew Smoothie 78
- Raspberry and Chocolate Cheesecake Smoothie 79
- Cinnamon Smoothie 80

CHAPTER NINE KETO APPETIZER RECIPES 81

- Cheesy Asparagus 83
- Crispy Salt and Pepper Spiced Tofu 84
- Avocado Tuna Melt Bites 86
- Fish Fingers 87
- Instant pot Shrimp in Garlic Sauce 88
- Cauliflower Cheese & Onion Croquettes 89
- Zucchini Patties 90
- Smoked Paprika Zucchini Chips 91
- Bacon Wrapped Cheese Sticks 92
- Chili and Rosemary Roasted Nuts 93
- Avocado Balls 94
- Italian Stuffed Mushrooms 95
- Crusty Cheddar 96
- Pistachio Crusted Sun-dried Tomato Goat Cheese Balls 97
- Coconut Tortillas 98
- Kale Stuffed Portobello Mushrooms 99
- Salmon Fat Bombs 100
- Kale and Bacon Chips 102
- Chocolate Peanut Butter Fat Bomb 103
- Antipasto Kebabs 104

CHAPTER TEN KETO SALAD RECIPES 105

- Keto Crack Slaw 107
- Sweet n Spicy Salad 108
- Mediterranean Chopped Salad 109
- Bacon Blue Zoodle Salad 110
- Healthy Cobb Salad 111
- Easy Keto Slaw 113
- Lemon Blueberry Chicken Salad 115
- Lobster Roll Salad 116
- Grilled Halloumi Salad 117
- Loaded Chicken Salad 118
- Balsamic Flat Iron Steak Salad 120
- Cheeseburger Salad 123

CHAPTER ELEVEN KETO LUNCH RECIPES 124

- Easy White Turkey Chili 126
- Spinach and Feta Turkey Burgers 127
- Eggplant and Bacon Alfredo 128
- Baked Chicken 129
- Tuna Bowl with Avocado and Noodle Rice 130
- Low Carb keto Lasagna 132
- Steak with Mushroom Port Sauce 134
- BBQ pulled Beef Sando 135
- Broccoli with Italian Sausage 137
- Enchilada style stuffed peppers 138
- Lemon herb Low Carb keto loaf 140
- Low Carb keto chili 141
- Super food meatballs 142
- Roasted Chicken Stacks 144
- Curry chicken lettuce wraps 146
- Lemon Balsamic Chicken with Zoodles 147
- Mexican Shredded Beef 149
- Creamy Mushroom Chicken 151
- Mushroom Bacon skillet 152
- Shrimp Stir Fry with baked cauliflower rice 153
- Low carb crispy fried chicken 155
- The perfect keto lunch 156
- Turkey Sausage Frittata 158

CHAPTER TWELVE KETO DINNER –RECIPES 159

- Creamy Tuscan Garlic Chicken 161

Grilled Chicken and Spinach Pizza 162
  Zucchini Pasta with Chicken & Pistachios 164
  Chicken Club Stuffed Avocadoes 166
  Kale and Turkey Sausage Sauté 167
  Zucchini Pizza Boats 168
  Leftover Turkey Casserole 171
  Jalapeño Cheddar Burgers 173
  Beef Satay and Peanut Sauce 174
  Garlic Butter Brazilian Steak 176
  Beef and Mushroom Stuffed Peppers 177
  Easy Steak Fajita 178
  Parmesan Crusted Pork Chops 180
  Sausage, Pepper and Cauliflower Fried Rice 181
  BBQ Pork Thai Style 183
  Pork Egg Roll in a Bowl 185
  Easy Pork Stir Fry 187
  Broiled Lamb and Butter Fennel 189
  Lamb Chops with Herb Butter 190
  Lamb Souvlaki (Greek Lamb Skewers) 191
  Turkish Lamb & Eggplant Kebabs 192
  Squid Noodle Pasta 194
  Tuna Fish Salad 195
  Bacon and Shrimp Risotto 197
  Seafood Chowder 198
  Shrimp Ceviche Stuffed Avocado 200

CHAPTER THIRTEEN KETO VEGETARIAN RECIPES 202
  Bell Pepper Basil Pizza 204
  Keto Noodle Bowls with Creamy Curry Sauce 206
  Sesame Tofu and Eggplant 208
  Loaded Cauliflower 210

CHAPTER FOURTEEN KETO SIDE DISHES 211
  Cauliflower Couscous 213
  Cauliflower Garlic Breadsticks 214
  Garlic Grilled Broccoli 215
  Easy Cheesy Zucchini Gratin 216
  Baked Parmesan Zucchini Rounds 217
  Creamy Mock Potato Mash 218
  Chinese Vegetable Stir-Fry 219

- Ginger and Garlic Bok Choy Stir-Fry 221
- Roasted Cauliflower Steaks 222

CHAPTER FIFTEEN KETO DESERTS 223
- Nutty Blackberry Fat Bombs 224
- Keto Vanilla Pound cake 225
- Mocha and Coconut Mug Cake 227
- Vegan Coconut Macaroons 228
- Easy Orange cake balls 229
- Raspberry Cheesecake in Chocolate 231
- Keto carrot cake with cream cheese frosting 232
- Keto avocado brownies 235
- Almond Joy Chia Pudding 237
- Avocado Popsicle with lime and coconut 238
- Chocolate coconut keto ice cream 239
- Peanut Butter Popsicles 240
- Low-Carb vanilla bean ice cream 241

CONCLUSION 242

INTRODUCTION

I want to thank you for choosing this book, *'Keto Diet – A Simple and Effective Guide to Losing Weight for Beginners,'* and hope you find the book informative and learn everything you need to know about the topic at hand – The Ketogenic diet.

I know that some of you are praying that this doesn't turn out to be another one of those crash diet books, which lead you nowhere. I am also aware that some of you are on the verge of giving up when it comes to fad diets. And that's a good thing. It's only when you decide to give up these so-called "diets' that I can introduce you to the ketogenic diet. I promise you that, after reading this book, you will feel much more hopeful about your overall health and weight loss issues.

Have you heard of the ketogenic diet? Do you know that it's easier to follow than you think? If all the information on the Internet and newspapers about the ketogenic diet is overwhelming you, you have stumbled onto the right guide. My intention to create this book was to educate my readers about everything they need to know about the ketogenic diet. Although this book is specially designed for beginners, it won't hurt to know more about this diet even if you are a pro.

One of the most obvious reasons why people take up the ketogenic diet is because of the weight loss results it offers. But that's not it. The ketogenic diet is much more than that, and you are about to unravel a whole load of other benefits that this diet offers. I sincerely hope that you will enjoy reading this book as much as I enjoyed creating it.

Happy reading!

CHAPTER ONE

THE KETOGENIC DIET AND ITS BENEFITS

When people hear about the ketogenic diet, the first thing that comes to their mind is "Does it work?" The answer is a big "Yes." The ketogenic diet works, and it works very well indeed. Before I go ahead and explain what the ketogenic diet has to offer, let us look at what the ketogenic diet is all about.

What is Keto?

The ketogenic diet is a low carb, high fat and moderate protein diet. The focus of this diet is to allow your body to get into a metabolic state called "Ketosis."

What is Ketosis?

Ketosis is a state that occurs when your body starts running out of glycogen stores (sugar). At this stage, your body starts looking for another source of fuel. When this happens, your liver starts processing fat into ketones, making them the primary source of fuel for the body.

To summarize, fat->ketones+energy

Now let's look at some of the most talked about benefits of this diet.

Weight loss

Isn't this the first thing people look for whenever they consider keto? Since fat becomes a primary source of fuel for the body, it actively starts burning fat instead of looking for glucose.

How does this happen?

When your body enters ketosis, both your insulin levels as well as blood pressure drop. This encourages the fat cells to release the water that they have been retaining, and this is the reason why most people experience a drastic amount of weight loss - due to loss of water.

After that, the fat cells become small enough to enter your bloodstream and the liver from where they get converted into ketones. This process continues to take place throughout your ketogenic journey as long as there is a calorie deficit.

Appetite control

Amazing things happen when you are on a low-carb diet like the keto diet. You will start feeling less hungry within days of following this diet. The random cravings which once caused you to be tempted to all the sinful things suddenly vanish. Once your appetite goes down, you will no longer feel like reaching for that jar of cookies or a bucket of fries. When you are on keto, you will naturally start feeling satiated without having to eat much.

A lot of people who take up the ketogenic diet are also capable of intermittent fasting since they only eat during a specific period of the day. So, if you are planning to take up fasting in the future, you will always get the upper hand. This is mainly possible because while on the ketogenic diet, your stomach isn't rumbling and thus dictating that you need a cupcake to feel full.

Better mental focus

Initially, you may find it difficult to have intense focus due to a slight drop in your energy when you start keto. But as the days go by, you will find that your focus is getting sharper and sharper. The problem with a diet that is full of carbs is it causes your blood sugar levels to rise and fall constantly. Since this kind of energy is non-consistent, it becomes difficult for your brain to focus for a longer duration.

When you are in the state of ketosis, your brain starts using ketones as fuel. This consistent supply of fuel helps the brain to focus more. Also, you won't experience brain fog. When you are eating carbs, chances are that you may often feel indecisive, making you incapable of making the right decisions. But once you get into ketosis, you will start noticing the difference.

More energy

Your body has a limited capacity to store glycogen, and because of this, you are required to refuel to maintain the energy levels constantly. That's why a lot of people are munching on something or tempted to eat during the whole day. With keto, your body has a lot of fat to work with. This also means that your body will stay in the state of ketosis for longer, making sure that it never runs out of energy.

Most people who take up the ketogenic diet start experiencing a sudden surge of energy. The high energy they feel spills over to other aspects of life, and they start to feel better about themselves. Can you imagine not having to take a nap after lunch? That's the kind of energy the ketogenic diet gives you.

Fights Type 2 diabetes

People who have Type 2 diabetes also suffer from elevated levels of insulin in the body. Since the ketogenic diet eliminates sugar from your diet, it helps to lower the Hb1Ac count in your body and can reverse Type 2 diabetes. Several studies have shown that following the ketogenic diet can drastically reduce the markers that are associated with Type 2 diabetes.

Increases HDL cholesterol

When people hear about HDL cholesterol, their first reaction is a state of panic. But what they don't know is that there are two types of cholesterol: the LDL and HDL.

HDL is the good type of cholesterol, which is known to carry the cholesterol away from the body and straight to the liver where it can be excreted or reused. On the other hand, LDL is known to carry the cholesterol to the rest of the body from the liver.

When you are on keto, the triglyceride levels in your body decrease, while HDL levels rise, having high HDL levels is an indicator of heart disease. The higher the triglyceride levels in the body, the greater the risk of developing heart disease.

Lowers blood pressure

Consistently elevated levels of blood pressure indicate future heart issues. The ketogenic diet does a marvelous job of decreasing your blood pressure levels.

Effective against metabolic syndrome

Metabolic syndrome is a condition that is linked to the risk of developing heart disease as well as diabetes.

Metabolic syndrome is a collection of various symptoms such as:

- Elevated blood pressure levels
- Abdominal obesity
- High triglycerides
- High fasting blood sugar levels
- Low good HDL cholesterol levels

The good thing is that the ketogenic diet is immensely effective in treating all these above-mentioned symptoms. Under a low-carb diet like the keto, all these conditions get almost eliminated.

Therapeutic for numerous brain disorders

Your brain requires glucose as a certain part of your brain can only burn this kind of sugar. This is also the reason why the liver starts producing glucose out of protein if you stop eating carbs. IN spite of this, a large part of your brain is capable of burning ketones, which get formed when the carb intake is low or when you are starving. This is the exact mechanism behind the ketogenic diet that the doctors have been using for decades to treat epilepsy in children who stop responding to drug treatment.

In numerous cases, the ketogenic diet has even cured epilepsy completely. In a particular study, more than six children experienced more than 50% reduction in their epilepsy symptoms, while 16% of became completely seizure-free. The keto, as well as the low-carb diet, is being studied for other brain conditions like Parkinson's disease and Alzheimer's.

CHAPTER TWO

KETOGENIC FOODS TO EAT AND AVOID

What foods are keto?

Foods that fit into the ketogenic diet are non-starchy veggies and low-carb high-fat foods. It also includes various protein sources. Below is a rough list of some of the most nutritious ketogenic foods, which can be fit into a meal plan.

Healthy ketogenic fats

- Avocado
- Seeds
- Olives
- Cacao
- Plant-based oils
- Nuts and nut butter
- Veggies and low-carb fruit

- All kinds of fresh herbs
- Strawberries and melons
- Nonstarchy veggies like broccoli, cauliflower, radishes, greens, zucchini, eggplant, tomato, green beans, cucumber, mushrooms, celery, bok choy, cabbage, artichoke, onions, beets and carrots.

Keto proteins

- Fatty fish like mackerel, salmon and herring
- Chicken with the skin on
- Pork, lamb, beef, bison and goat
- Shellfish
- Organ meats
- Cheese, cottage cheese and unsweetened yogurt

Keto sweeteners

- Stevia
- Monk fruit
- Erythritol
- Other artificial sweeteners

Which foods are not keto?

A ketogenic meal plan is all about eating enough macros, and this means that you can fit in just about any type of foods in this plan except for high carb foods. There are several sources of carbs, which will push your daily limits within a single serving. Below is a list of foods that need to be avoided while on keto.

High Carb foods

- Milk
- Desserts
- Corn
- Potatoes
- Lentils, beans and legume
- Pasta, bread and all grains
- Soda and juice
- Dried fruit and most fruit
- Fried foods and breaded foods
- Sugars: honey, agave, maple, table sugar, etc.

Keto beverages

- Coffee and tea, unsweetened
- Water
- Club soda/sparkling water
- Artificially sweetened beverages
- Green vegetable juices and wheatgrass
- Flavored water with no added sugar

Low carb alcohol

- Light beers
- Wine and champagne
- Bourbon and scotch
- Gin, rum and vodka

CHAPTER THREE

SEVEN WAYS TO GET INTO KETOSIS

Choosing a ketogenic diet could mean changing your whole life for the better. For most people, starting the ketogenic diet isn't the hardest part, but getting into ketosis is.

The process of reaching the state of ketosis might seem like a long one. For some, it can take about a week to get into ketosis completely. But, what if you could speed up this process a little bit? Would you? Let's look at some of the ways we can quicken this process.

Cut down on carbs

This is one is a little obvious as the ketogenic diet is going to make you eliminate carbs from your diet anyway. That said, a lot of people seem to struggle with the entire concept of the ketogenic diet right from the beginning. The number of carbs some of our daily foods have will surprise you.

People can cut down on the high sugar ingredients like soda or candy or desserts pretty easily, but when it comes to eliminating foods like potatoes or pasta, they often struggle. The sooner you can cut down these items from your regular diet, the faster your body can eliminate all the glucose it uses for fuel. It is only then that your body starts turning into a fat burning machine. This small but effective step can go a long way toward ensuring that you get into the state of ketosis faster than expected.

Increase the intake of MCT's

Medium Chain Triglycerides are nothing but a type of fatty acid. These acids don't necessarily cause your insulin levels to rise, but they can easily be converted into ketones. MCT's can be found in the form of oils. These oils can be easily consumed by adding them to your meals, juices or even shakes. MCT's can speed up the process of getting into ketosis if you follow them up correctly with a perfect ketogenic diet plan.

It is vital that you consume as many macros as possible throughout your ketogenic diet journey, especially during the initial phase. If you fall off track for even the slightest time, you will end up delaying ketosis even longer.

Increase your fat intake

When following the ketogenic diet, you are going to be consuming a lot of fats. Unlike the popular belief that fats are bad for you, you need to consume enough fats to lose fat. This may sound a little weird but stay with me on this.

You need to ensure that you are consuming enough healthy fats for your body to be able to burn fats. What are healthy fats? The ones you get from coconut oil, olive oil, butter, etc. Do not consume processed oils under any circumstance as they are full of ingredients you don't need while on keto. Fewer carbs and more fats mean you are on your way to losing all of your body fat.

Watch your protein consumption

Since you won't be consuming any carbs on this diet, you may go overboard with your protein intake. This may sound good, but it can be harmful in the long run. Excessive protein can take a toll on your kidney function. When you consume excessive protein, the extra amount starts getting converted into glucose, which will get you back to where you started.

In the absence of this balance, you may experience increased insulin levels in the body, which may promote fat storage, and this is far from what you want.

Listen to your body

Your body is always sending you signals about what it wants and what it doesn't. Start listening. From the time you wake up, you need to listen to what your body is trying to tell you. If you are hungry, your stomach may start making those rumbling sounds, indicating that it needs fuel in the form of food. At the same time, if you are feeling full, you may not want to eat anything. It's that simple!

It is equally important to understand the difference between dehydration and hunger, because a lot of times, you may confuse the two and end up stuffing yourself with food when in reality you are not hungry. The next time you feel hungry, take a minute and observe whether you are hungry or just thirsty? If you drink a glass of water and don't feel hungry anymore, then you were just dehydrated.

Fast

If you have never tried fasting, you should give it a try. The more food we consume, the more difficult it becomes for the body to break it down. If you stay away from food for a certain amount of time, it can allow your body to break down the food and aid digestion easily. Also, going without food for longer periods means that your body will start using the extra fuel until the next meal. This also means that it can become easier to start burning off all the extra glucose lying in your system.

Don't forget to keep yourself hydrated throughout this process. Not hydrating yourself enough can cause a significant amount of complication in the body and you want to avoid that at all costs.

Workout

Working out is a great way to get into ketosis. While working out, you will be burning the glucose at a much faster pace. This will also speed up your weight loss even when you aren't on keto. Incredible, isn't it? If you are consuming enough macros and working out regularly, your body is going to get into ketosis much faster. You may experience a slight dip in the performance at the start, but your performance will start increasing at a steady pace once your body starts burning fat.

CHAPTER FOUR

DEBUNKING KETOGENIC DIET MYTHS

The ketogenic diet differs drastically from the standard "healthy diet" that people are obsessing over. This diet, which is low in carbs and high in fat, contradicts pretty much everything you may have heard about healthy eating. So, it's natural for people to assume that this diet could be dangerous in a lot of ways. Of course, the reality is far from these myths, but what people don't ask is whether there is any scientific evidence to these myths. In short, there aren't any. The ketogenic diet is in no way quackery and if anything, it is pure science. The medical profession designed this diet almost a century ago for treating epilepsy in children. Today, there are numerous studies that prove that the ketogenic diet has a lot of benefits to offer, the major one being weight loss.

All that said and done, if you are still a little skeptical about whether you should follow the ketogenic diet or not, let us help you debunk certain myths surrounding it.

You cannot live without carbohydrates

Although your body runs mainly on carbohydrates as a source of energy, these are not an essential nutrient. Your body can survive perfectly and thrive even without them. But when it comes to fats and proteins, it's a different story. Both fats, as well as proteins, are made of essential amino acids that are vital for normal health, and its functioning.

So, why is it that nutritionists and medical experts emphasize the need for carbohydrate consumption and talk as if one can't live without them? One reason could be because we are used to consuming carbs, and also because not every expert has a proper understanding of energy metabolism.

What is energy metabolism? It is the process of producing energy (ATP out of macronutrients such as proteins, carbs and fats.) When you consume these nutrients on a daily basis, your body starts favoring carbohydrates for energy production and uses the other two nutrients for enzyme production, tissue building and storage.

But even if you consume fewer carbs, your body is perfectly capable of using proteins and fats for energy. It starts breaking down proteins to produce a small amount of glucose using gluconeogenesis. Further, it breaks down the fatty acids present in the body to make keto bodies that can replace glucose in the muscles, brain and heart.

Keto is dangerous

Keto is a metabolic switch from how your body generally functions, but that doesn't mean that the ketogenic diet is dangerous. Several medical experts agree that ketosis is a very natural metabolic process. Moreover, recent research has shown that ketosis offers a range of health benefits

Being in ketosis is not only healthy, but it can accelerate weight loss to a large extent. So, why do people still believe in the dangers of keto? One reason could be because ketosis is sometimes confused for ketoacidosis. Now, what is ketoacidosis? It's a state of having dramatically elevated levels of ketones in the blood, which can make your blood acidic. This type of condition is common amongst people who suffer from alcoholism or Type 2 diabetes. Ketoacidosis is a direct result of faulty insulin functioning, which has no association with the ketogenic diet

Keto can cause nutrient deficiencies

When you are on keto, you avoid eating foods that are generally found in abundance such as fruit, veggies, legumes, whole grains, etc. All of these foods are considered to be high in nutrition, so when you exclude them while the following keto, it is believed to create nutritional deficiencies. However, the fact remains opposed to this belief. When the ketogenic diet is well planned, it can offer you all the essential nutrients that your body craves for. The ketogenic diet can keep you nourished, healthy and well functioning just like any other healthy diet and no, you won't be missing out on any nutrients. That said, there are a couple of weak spots with regards to keto nutrition. The following nutrients are difficult to get on this diet:

Fiber

Fiber can be obtained only from plant-based foods. This particular nutrient is extremely important for your gut to be able to function normally. When on keto, you satiate your fiber requirements with plenty of leafy greens, avocados, nuts, berries, and seeds. Fiber can also be taken as a dietary supplement.

Vitamin C

Adults require anywhere between 90 mg and 120 mg vitamin C dosage every day. One full cup of broccoli florets that contain merely 3.6 g of carbs can offer you even more than that. Among the other keto-friendly vitamin C sources include spinach, strawberries, and avocados. If you consume any of these items regularly, you will never have to worry about getting enough vitamin C.

Flavonoids

Flavonoids are plant-based compounds which act as antioxidants in your daily diet. Most plant-based foods are rich in flavonoids. So, as long as you are eating at least some amount of plant-based foods, you can get enough flavonoids.

A lot of dieters even worry about the ketogenic diet causing magnesium deficiencies. Again, this is not true. On keto, you will be eating plenty of nuts, seeds and leafy greens that are rich in magnesium.

Keto can cause calculus

Another myth that has been aggressively believed about the ketogenic diet is that it can cause calculus – a term for gallstones and kidney stones. Since the ketogenic diet is completely different to our normal diet, some people believe that it can get too overwhelming for the body to handle, ultimately causing calculus. This belief does not have any scientific backing.

Firstly, kidney stones develop due to following diets that are high in sodium, refined carbs and animal protein and oxalate foods. The ketogenic diet is low in carbs, oxalates and sodium, so there's no reason to blame it for your kidney issues. A commonly found cause of kidney stones is dehydration. And people often miss out on hydrating themselves well during the first week of the ketogenic journey since they lose a lot of electrolytes and water. But if you already know how the ketogenic diet works, and make sure that you keep yourself well hydrated, your risk of developing kidney stones due to dehydration goes down drastically.

As far as gallstones are concerned, many people suffer from asymptomatic gallstones. These stones are linked to genetic and not to low-carb and high-fat diets like the keto.

Keto increases the risk of heart disease

Coronary heart disease has been plaguing the world over the past few years. It's one of the leading causes of death across the globe. For a long time, most researchers believed that this disease could be a result of consuming excessive fat. But the recent research shows that the triggers are much more complex than that.

A recent and growing study suggests that refined carbohydrates could be the reason for the increase in CHD risk. The role of saturated fats is being studied further. They are known to have a special role in the biological function of humans, so skipping them is not going to be beneficial.

Besides, fat is also an important nutrient. It provides energy to the body regulates your body temperature as well as protects your organs. Fats also forms the membranes of the cells, contains vitamins as well as some fat which act as hormones. Omega 3 fatty acids, as well as unsaturated fats, offer several health benefits and protection against diseases such as cancer, heart disease and depression.

Low-fat diets, on the other hand, are making people gain weight and develop metabolic diseases. This is happening because people tend to compensate for the lack of fats in their diets by consuming excess carbs.

CHAPTER FIVE

KETO TIPS FOR BEGINNERS

Are looking to give this low-carb, high fat and moderate protein diet a whirl? Before you proceed, you need to know these valuable tips that will help you stick to the ketogenic diet for a lot longer than you imagined.

Ease into the ketogenic diet by adding more fats

Are you a heavy carb eater? Is yes, then don't jump your guns and start following the ketogenic diet before you have eased yourself into it. Going from your regular dietary habits to a fully-fledged ketogenic diet is going to be a big shock to your entire system. There's a name for it. Have you heard of the keto flu? Why do people get keto flu? Because they drastically switch their dietary habits to start the ketogenic diet. Instead, if you start upping your fat intake for about seven days before starting the ketogenic diet, the journey could get much easier for you. Get some healthy fats in your meals such as coconut oil or avocados. These resources of fat will prepare your liver, gallbladder and your entire digestive system for what's coming next. You can feel free to eat an avocado toast sandwich almost every single day during the week before taking up keto.

Start using low-carb ingredients to prepare your meals

Taking up the ketogenic diet doesn't mean that you will have to give up on pizza, fries, hamburgers or pasta. All you need to do is make clever swaps. Don't know how? Here's how. You can simple make zucchini noodles or spaghetti squash instead of consuming the carb-y noodles you get at the restaurants. Similarly, you can use cauliflower as a base in your pizza instead of refined flour. Desserts can be made out of fruit, or you can bake your fries or eat burgers that contain veggie patties that are made out of carrots, sweet potato and French beans. There are a lot of ways you can satisfy your cravings for your favorite foods without loading up on calories. All you need to do is think a little outside the box.

Add herbs to your drinks to combat sugar cravings

Since you are supposed to steer clear of sugar while on keto, chances are that you are feeling disappointed because you aren't able to indulge your sweet tooth in sugary desserts. But there's a solution for this too. You can replace the refined sugar with some high-flavored herbs like cinnamon, licorice root or cardamom powder. You can sprinkle these herbs into your tea, coffee, shakes and even desserts. Now, I agree that these herbs are not exactly sweet, but they will certainly make your drinks taste better. Want a snacking option? Get your hands on some super satiating fat balls. A word of caution: even though the use of Stevia is allowed on the keto diet, don't overdo it.

Keep your energy up by hydrating yourself well

Needless to say, that the drastic elimination of carbohydrates from your diet is going to make your energy levels go down. But you can always compensate it by hydrating yourself well. Drinking at least 3-4 liters of water especially during the initial stage of the ketogenic diet can give a natural boost to your energy and help your body to transition. You can also sip on some juice and green tea. Make sure you aren't gulping down too many cups of juice as the sugar levels present in fruit can cause a problem. But you can always load up on some matcha-tea or some super-herbs like holy basil, ashwagandha or Cordyceps, which can help fight stress and fatigue.

Sleep well

In the initial phase of keto, a lot of people complain of not being able to sleep properly. When you start introducing your body to different foods in varying amounts, the body starts transitioning from using glucose to create energy to burning fat. This also makes you experience dizzyingly high levels of energy throughout the day. These changes can keep you awake at night, but fortunately, there are ways to combat this situation.

- Be mindful of your blood sugar. Make sure that you aren't overeating or snacking during bedtime. Replace it with something light and easy which can soothe your hunger without interrupting your sleep.

- Keep varying your veggies. Certain veggies like Brussels sprouts, kale and cabbage can often cause gas. Instead of eating them for dinner, have them for lunch.

- Get as many minerals in as you can. Essential electrolytes such as magnesium, potassium and sodium can calm your nervous system down.

- Ensure that your melatonin productions not hindered. Tart cherry juice contains the highest concentration of melatonin, so feel free to sip on it multiple times during the day.

Don't overdo your workouts

The first few weeks of the keto diet are heavier on both your mind and on your body. If you don't take the necessary care, it can also weigh heavily on your emotions, causing them to spin out of control. That's also why a lot of people feel irritable and experience extreme mood swings when they first start following the keto diet. Especially the first three days of the keto diet are when most people feel the weakest. During this phase, you should keep your exercise schedule to the minimum, if at all. If you do wish to exercise every day, you can indulge in some light activities such as walking for 20 minutes a day or yoga. You can also practice deep breathing exercises during the first few days. You can certainly get back to lifting weights, running, spinning or cross fit after a couple of weeks have passed by, but until then, take it easy.

Going on the ketogenic diet can seem like a nightmare, but it's not forever

Okay, I went a little overboard with that point, but seriously, I know a lot of people who may feel overwhelmed by the experience during the initial week or so. This is not to discourage you from taking up keto, but it's important that you plan your transition well. For instance, don't start with the keto diet when you are particularly stressed or on weekdays, and clear your kitchen of all the junk food and sugary drinks before you start. The initial transition from your regular meals to the ketogenic diet meals can be a difficult one indeed. But the good news is that it doesn't have to be forever. If you are patient with yourself and follow all the instructions correctly during the first two weeks, it will only get easier and easier from then.

CHAPTER SIX

KETO BREAKFAST RECIPES

AVOCADO BREAKFAST BOWL

Makes 1 servings

Ingredients

1 large avocado

1 tablespoon unsalted butter

3 large eggs

3 bacon rashers, sliced into pieces

¼ teaspoon salt

A pinch of ground black pepper for taste

Instructions

1. Wash the avocado properly and pat it dry using a paper towel. Now using a knife, cut the avocado into two halves and gently scoop out the flesh with the help of a spoon.

2. Place a large pan on the stove on medium heat. Add some butter and allow it to melt. While the butter is melting away, crack open the eggs in a bowl, add some salt and pepper and beat them.

3. Add the bacon slices on the pan and sauté them for 2-3 minutes until nice and brown.

4. Remove the bacon and add the eggs to the pan and keep stirring them as they scramble. The eggs shouldn't take more than 5 minutes to cook. After about 2 minutes, as the eggs are cooking away, add the bacon and scramble the mixture together so it blends well.

5. Remove it in a large bowl.

6. Fill a bit of this mixture into both the Avocado halves.

7. Sprinkle some salt and pepper on top and serve them.

CHORIZO SHAKSHUKA

Makes 3 servings

Ingredients

½ lb ground chorizo

5 cloves garlic, minced

1 small onion, chopped

1 small red bell pepper, chopped

3 large eggs

1 ounce queso fresco, crumbled

1 ½ teaspoons paprika

1 ½ teaspoons ground cumin

¾ teaspoon crushed red pepper flakes or chili powder

Salt to taste

Pepper to taste

Instructions

over medium heat. Add oil. When the oil melts, add
ok until brown.

a slotted spoon and set aside on a plate.

ack on heat. Add onions, bell pepper and garlic and sauté
e translucent.

lt and pepper. Sauté for a few seconds until fragrant.

shed red pepper and tomatoes with its juice and mash
atoes. Taste and adjust the seasoning if necessary.

s in the mixture. Crack an egg into each cavity. Cover and
eggs are cooked as per your desire.

eat. Sprinkle queso fresco and cilantro and serve.

½ tablespoon coconut oil

1 can (14 ounces) diced tomatoes with its juice

A handful fresh cilantro, chopped to garnish

KETO MEXICAN SCRAMBLED EGGS

Makes 4 servings

Ingredients

6 large eggs

1 scallion

2 pickled jalapenos

1 large tomato

3 oz. shredded cheese

2 tablespoons butter

½ teaspoon salt

½ teaspoon ground black pepper

Instructions

1. For starters, wash the tomato thoroughly under some running water and pat it dry using paper towels. Using a sharp knife, finely chop the tomato. Similarly, chop the jalapenos and scallion.

2. Add the jalapeno chilies and scallions and sauté for about a minute.

3. Throw in them chopped tomato and cook for another 2 minutes until slightly tender.

4. While the tomato is cooking away, in a bowl, gently crack open the eggs and beat them lightly using a fork. Make sure that the mixture isn't too frothy.

5. Pour this liquid into the pan, add some cheese on top and cover with a lid.

6. Cook it for about 3-4 minutes.

7. Transfer on a large plate, seasoning it with some salt, pepper and a little more cheese if you wish.

8. Serve.

KETO FRIED EGGS WITH KALE AND PORK

Makes 2 servings

Ingredients

½ lb. fresh kale

3 oz. butter

6 oz. bacon or smoked pork belly

¼ cup frozen cranberries

1 oz. walnuts or pecans

4 large eggs

½ teaspoon salt

½ teaspoon ground black pepper

Instructions

1. Wash the kale bunch thoroughly under some running water and pat it dry using paper towels. Using a sharp kitchen knife, slice up the kale leaves into large squares. Keep aside.

2. Place a large pan on the stove on medium heat. Add some butter and allow it to melt.

3. Add the kale leaves and turn the flame on high. Fry the kale until it nice and crispy from both sides. Remove it in a dish.

4. Now throw in the bacon or the pork bell in the same pan and fry it from each side for about 2-3 minutes until it nice and brown. Make sure you don't burn the bacon. To avoid, keep turning the bacon slices often.

5. Now lower the flame, and add the sautéed kale to the pan and stir using a large wooden spoon.

6. Sprinkle some salt and pepper and mix again.

7. Add the nuts and the cranberries, toss all the ingredients and cook for about 1 minute until slightly warmed and tender. Set aside in a bowl.

8. Now turn up the heat and in the meanwhile, gently crack open the eggs straight onto the pan. You can sprinkle some more salt and pepper on it and fry them for a couple of minutes.

9. Now, place the greens on a large plate and then place each of the fried eggs one besides the other.

10. Serve immediately.

CAULIFLOWER AND KALE FRITTATA IN AN INSTANT POT

Makes 2 servings

Ingredients

1 tablespoon extra-virgin olive oil, divided

1 cup cauliflower florets, chopped into small pieces

2 ½ cups kale, chopped

½ teaspoon fresh thyme, chopped

Salt to taste

Pepper to taste

¼ teaspoon smoked paprika

1 small onion, sliced

2 cloves garlic, minced

4 large eggs

¼ cup goat's cheese, crumbled or Manchego cheese, shredded

Instructions

1. Press 'Sauté' button. Add oil. When the oil is heated, add onions and sauté until light brown.

2. Add cauliflower and sauté for a couple of minutes.

3. Add garlic and sauté for a few seconds until fragrant. Add kale, salt, pepper and thyme and stir until kale wilts. Press 'Cancel' button.

4. Add eggs, paprika, salt and pepper into a bowl. Whisk well. Pour into the pot.

5. Close the lid. Select 'Steam' Button. Set the timer for 12-15 minutes.

6. When done, slice into wedges and serve.

KETO SEAFOOD OMELETTE

Makes 2 servings

Ingredients

2 tablespoons olive oil

5 oz. seafood mix or shrimp

1 red chili pepper

2 garlic cloves

½ teaspoon fennel seeds

½ cup mayonnaise

1 tablespoon dried or fresh chives

6 large eggs

2 tablespoons butter or olive oil

½ teaspoon salt

½ teaspoon ground black pepper

Instructions

1. Clean the shrimps properly using paper towels. Remove the tail. Fill a pot with a little bit of water and bring it to a boil. Add the shrimps and cook them for about 15-20 minutes until they are tender. Make sure you don't overcook them otherwise they may turn out to be chewy. Allow it to cool off and drain the excess water.

2. Preheat the broiler.

3. Broil the cooked shrimp along with chili, fennel, minced garlic, salt, pepper and cumin and allow it to cool off once done. Let it come to room temperature.

4. In a bowl, gently crack open the eggs one by one and whisk it using a fork. You can also use a blender to whisk them. Add some salt and pepper and whisk lightly once again.

5. Heat a non-stick pan on medium flame. Now pour the egg mixture and fry the eggs with some butter or oil for about 3 minutes.

6. Transfer the omelette on a large plate. Now fill the seafood mixture inside the omelette and fold it using your hands. You can also use a toothpick to secure it.

7. Serve along with some tahini sauce.

KETO EGG MUFFINS

Makes 6 servings

Ingredients

12 large eggs

2 scallions, finely chopped

5 oz. bacon

6 oz. shredded cheese

2 tablespoons green or red pesto

1 teaspoon salt

1 teaspoon ground black pepper

Instructions

1. Preheat the oven to 350 degrees F.

2. Grease the muffin molds with some oil or butter and set them aside. Using a knife, finely chop the scallions and set them aside too.

3. Heat a pan on medium flame and then add the bacon slices to it. Cook them for about 3 minutes on each side until they are nice and brown. Just make sure you don't burn them.

4. Now add the cooked bacon at the bottom of the tin along with the chopped scallions. You can also crumble the bacon a bit using your hands and place it in the tin.

5. In a bowl, gently crack open the eggs one by one and whisk it using a fork. You can also use a blender to whisk them. Add some salt and pepper, pesto and whisk lightly once again.

6. Pour the egg batter carefully on top of the bacon.

7. Place the muffin tins inside the oven and bake for about 20 minutes until they are completely done.

8. Allow them to cool off for 2-3 minutes and serve.

STRAWBERRY CHOCOLATE CREPES

Makes 2 servings

Ingredients

3 large eggs

3 tablespoons coconut flour

2 drops of Stevia

1 tablespoon psyllium husk powder

1/3 cup water

For the filling

1 oz. dark chocolate

½ tablespoon organic coconut oil

½ cup fresh strawberries

Instructions

1. Wash the strawberries thoroughly under some running water and dry them up by placing them on paper towels. Using a knife, roughly chop them up and set aside.

2. IN a bowl, crack the eggs carefully and whisk them using a fork. To this, add some coconut flour, psyllium husk powder, and sweetener and mix again.

3. Boil some water in a vessel and add it to the egg mixture until it is well incorporated.

4. Add one tablespoon oil on a non-stick pan and twirl it around. Once the pan is hot, pour about ¼ of the crepe liquid and lower the flame. Allow it to cook for 3 minutes until golden brown and flip it over. Cook for another 2 minutes and transfer on a plate. Repeat the same process with the remaining batter.

5. Fold these crepes and make them into a roll.

6. Melt some chocolate over double boiler along with some butter or coconut oil and pour it over the crepes.

7. Add a handful of chopped berries on top and serve.

INSTANT POT CAULIFLOWER HASH BROWN CASSEROLE

Makes 4 servings

Ingredients

6 eggs

4 cups cauliflower, shredded

¼ cup milk

Salt to taste

Pepper to taste

½ teaspoon dry mustard

1 small onion, chopped

1 cup cheddar cheese, shredded

5 ounces cooked sausages, crumbled or sliced

Cooking spray

Instructions

1. Whisk together eggs, milk, salt, pepper, and mustard in a bowl.

2. Spray inside of the cooking pot with cooking spray.

3. Spread half the cauliflower at the bottom of the pot. Sprinkle salt and pepper over it.

4. Layer with half the sausages followed by half the cheese.

5. Repeat the above 2 steps once more. Pour egg mixture over it.

6. Close the lid. Press 'Slow cook' button and set the timer for 4 hours.

7. Serve hot or warm.

LEMON AND BLUEBERRY MUFFINS

Makes 10 yields servings

Ingredients

4 whole eggs

¾ cup coconut milk, full-fat

1 teaspoon vanilla extract

1 cup collagen protein powder

½ cup coconut flour

1 ½ tablespoons birch xylitol

1 teaspoon baking powder

½ teaspoon xanthan gum

1/8 teaspoon pink salt

3 tablespoons unsalted butter

¾ cup blueberries

For the lemon glaze

1 small lemon, zested and juiced

Instructions

1. Preheat the oven to 350 degrees F.

2. IN a bowl, crack the eggs and whisk them together along with vanilla ns coconut milk. You can also use a hand blender to whisk them.

3. Now add coconut flour, xylitol, some collagen protein powder, xanthan gum, and baking powder, salt and whisk again. Gently fold in the butter. At this point, you will have a very thick and gooey batter.

4. Stir in the strawberries and mix with a spoon.

5. Grease the muffin molds with some butter and add the egg batter into each of these without spilling it.

6. Place the muffin molds on a baking tray and then place the tray inside the oven.

7. Bake for about 20 minutes until the muffins are completely cooked you can insert a toothpick to check if they are done. Remove the molds from the oven and allow them to cool off for about 10 minutes.

8. Start preparing the lemon glaze by mixing the sweetener with lemon juice and lemon zest and mix well.

5 tablespoons powdered birch xylitol

9. Remove the muffins from the molds, place them in a plate pour the lemon glaze on top and serve immediately.

ROSEMARY BAGELS

Makes 4 servings

Ingredients

1 ½ cups almond flour

¾ teaspoon baking soda

¾ teaspoon xanthan gum

3 tablespoons psyllium husk powder

1 egg

3 egg whites

¼ teaspoon salt

½ cup warm water

Some avocado oil

1 tablespoon rosemary, chopped

Instructions

1. Preheat the oven to 250 degrees F.
2. IN a bowl, combine some almond flour, salt, baking soda and xanthan gum and mix well.
3. IN a bowl, crack open the eggs and whisk them along with some warm water. Add the husk and mix well so there are no lumps. You can also use a hand blender to whisk the mixture.
4. Add all the liquid ingredients to the dry mixture.
5. Now brush the bagel mold with some avocado oil.
6. Gently press the dough into the mold using your hands.
7. Sprinkle some fresh rosemary on top.
8. Place the bagel molds in the oven and bake them for 45 minutes. You can use a toothpick to check its doneness. Allow them to cool off about 15 minutes.
9. Take the bagels off the mold and serve.

INSTANT POT MELAMEN

Makes 6 servings

Ingredients

3 cups onions, chopped

3 cups green bell peppers, chopped

4 large tomatoes, chopped

2 tablespoons extra virgin olive oil

2 eggs, beaten

Pepper powder to taste

Salt to taste

Instructions

1. Press 'Sauté' button. Add oil. When the oil is heated, add bell pepper and sauté for a couple of minutes.

2. Add onions and sauté until the onions are translucent.

3. Add tomatoes, salt and pepper and stir well. Press 'Cancel' button.

4. Pour egg over the veggies. Do not stir.

5. Close the lid. Press 'Steam' button and set the timer for 10 minutes.

6. Serve with cucumbers and feta cheese

CHAPTER SEVEN

KETO SOUP RECIPES

HOT AND SOUR VEGETABLE SOUP

Makes 4-6 servings

Ingredients

1 ½ tablespoons olive oil

2 teaspoons ginger, grated

1 medium carrot, chopped

1 medium sweet potato, peeled, cubed

1 medium red bell pepper, chopped

1 small zucchini, chopped

2 cups Savoy cabbage, chopped

2 baby Bok Choy, thinly sliced

7 ounces canned diced tomatoes

1 medium onion, thinly sliced

1 jalapeño, minced

5 cups vegetable broth or water

3 tablespoons rice vinegar

Instructions

1. Place a heavy bottomed pot over medium heat. Add oil. When the oil is heated, add onions, ginger and chilies and sauté until onions are translucent.

2. Add sweet potatoes and carrots. Cover and cook for 5 minutes.

3. Add cabbage and cook for 1-2 minutes. Add broth and bring to the boil.

4. Lower heat and simmer for 5 minutes. Add zucchini, bell pepper and tofu. Cook until the vegetables are soft.

5. Add soy sauce, vinegar, salt, pepper and arrowroot mixture stirring constantly. Stir until the soup thickens.

6. Add Bok Choy and canned tomatoes and cook until the Bok Choy wilts.

7. Add sesame oil. Stir and remove from heat.

8. Serve in soup bowls.

¼ cup soy sauce or coconut aminos

Salt to taste

Pepper to taste

1 teaspoon sesame oil

2 tablespoons arrowroot powder mixed with ¼ cup water

4 ounces extra firm tofu, cut into ½ inch pieces

CHICKEN MUSHROOM SOUP IN AN INSTANT POT

Makes 6 servings

Ingredients

1 large onion, thinly sliced

3 cups mushrooms, chopped

1 ½ lbs chicken breast, skinless, boneless, chopped into large chunks

Pepper to taste

Salt to taste

1 ½ teaspoons Italian seasoning or poultry seasoning

5 cloves garlic, minced

1 ½ yellow squash, chopped

4 cups chicken stock

¾ cup heavy whipping cream (optional)

Instructions

1. Add all the ingredients except cream into the instant pot.

2. Close the lid. Press 'Manual' button and set the timer for 15 minutes.

3. When the cook time is over, let the pressure release naturally for 10 minutes after which quick release excess pressure.

4. Remove the chicken with a slotted spoon and place on your cutting board. When cool enough to handle, shred with a pair of forks.

5. Using an immersion blender, blend the soup in the instant pot.

6. Add chicken and cream and stir.

7. Ladle into soup bowls and serve

CREAMY SPINACH SOUP

Makes 2 servings

Ingredients

8 cups spinach, chopped

4 cloves garlic, sliced

2 cups water

1 cup coconut milk, unsweetened

1 medium onion, chopped

½ cup heavy cream

6 tablespoons butter, unsalted

¼ teaspoon pepper powder

¼ teaspoon salt

2 tablespoons cream cheese

Instructions

1. Place a saucepan over low heat. Add butter and melt. Add garlic and sauté until fragrant. Add onion and sauté until translucent.

2. Add spinach and cook until it wilts.

3. Add water and boil.

4. Remove from heat and cool for a while. Blend with an immersion blender until smooth.

5. Place the saucepan back on heat. Heat thoroughly.

6. Remove from heat. Add cream and milk and mix.

7. Ladle into soup bowls.

8. Top with cream cheese and serve immediately.

CHICKEN SOUP

Makes 4 servings

Ingredients

½ lb chicken, cleaned, rinsed

½ tablespoons chicken soup powder

1 teaspoon garlic powder

1 medium zucchini, grated

1 medium carrot, peeled, grated

1 medium onion, chopped into chunks

4 cups water or chicken stock

1 teaspoon turmeric powder

1 tablespoon fresh dill

Salt to taste

Pepper to taste

Instructions

1. Place a soup pot over medium heat. Add stock or water and let it boil.

2. Add chicken, onion, garlic powder, soup powder, dill, turmeric, salt and pepper.

3. Let it cook until chicken is tender. Remove the chicken pieces from the saucepan with a slotted spoon and set aside on a plate. When cool enough to handle, shred the chicken and add it back to the pot

4. Add zucchini and carrot and simmer for 8-10 minutes.

5. Ladle into soup bowls and serve.

INSTANT POT LOW CARB TACO SOUP

Makes 4 servings

Ingredients

1 lb ground beef

2 cloves garlic, minced

1 teaspoon ground cumin

10 ounces canned diced tomatoes with chilies

¼ cup heavy cream

½ tablespoon onion flakes (optional)

1 tablespoon chili powder

4 ounces cream cheese

16 ounces beef broth

Salt to taste

Pepper to taste

Optional toppings:

Sour cream

Instructions

1. Press 'Sauté' button. Press 'Adjust' button once. Add ground beef. Sauté until it is brown. Add spices, garlic, onion flakes, tomatoes, beef broth and salt. Mix well.

2. Close the lid. Press 'Soup' button and set the timer for 5 minutes.

3. When the cook time is over, let the pressure release naturally for 10 minutes after which quick release excess pressure. Stir well.

4. Add cream cheese and heavy cream and mix well.

5. Ladle into soup bowls and serve with optional toppings.

Jalapeno peppers, sliced

Few black olives, sliced

4 tablespoons cheddar cheese, shredded

THAI COCONUT SOUP

Makes 4 servings

Ingredients

For Thai coconut soup:

5 chicken breasts, cut into thin strips and then into 1 inch pieces

3 tablespoons Thai garlic chili paste

5 tablespoons fish sauce

1 ½ tablespoons coconut aminos

2 cups coconut milk

2 teaspoons fresh ginger, peeled, minced

2 ½ cups chicken stock or broth

4 cups water

2 teaspoons lemon juice or to taste

Salt to taste

Instructions

1. To make Thai coconut soup: Add all the ingredients for Thai coconut soup into a soup pot. Place soup pot over medium heat. Simmer until chicken is cooked through.

Pepper to taste

3 sprigs Thai fresh basil

Fresh cilantro leaves, chopped to garnish

CHICKEN AND BACON SOUP

Makes 7 servings

Ingredients

2 slices bacon, chopped

1 small onion, chopped

2 tablespoons sundried tomatoes, chopped

4 cups chicken stock

1 cup celery root or jicama or turnip or radish, peeled, cut into ½ inch cubes

1 cup yellow squash, sliced, quartered

2 cups Swiss chard, chopped

Salt to taste

Pepper to taste

½ tablespoon olive oil

½ tablespoon garlic, minced

½ cup white mushrooms, sliced

Instructions

1. Place a soup pot over medium heat. Add oil. When the oil is heated, add bacon and cook for a couple of minutes.

2. Add onions and garlic and sauté for a couple of minutes. Add sundried tomatoes and mushrooms and sauté for 4-5 minutes.

3. Add water, stock, chicken and celery root. Lower heat and simmer for 10 minutes.

4. Add squash, sugar snap peas and Swiss chard. Cook for 10 minutes.

5. Add red wine vinegar, salt and pepper. Stir well.

6. Ladle into soup bowls. Garnish with basil and serve immediately.

1 ½ cups water

2 cups cooked chicken breast, chopped

½ cup sugar snap peas, cut into 1 inch pieces

A handful fresh basil, chopped

1 tablespoon red wine vinegar

THAI CURRY SOUP WITH TOFU

Makes 8 servings

Ingredients

2 onions, minced

2 cloves garlic, minced

2 cups small cauliflower florets

3 cups small broccoli florets

6 cups water

2 teaspoons chicken or vegetable bouillon powder

4 tablespoons Thai green curry paste or to taste

32 ounces firm or extra firm tofu, chopped into small cubes

½ bell pepper, cut into strips

1 1/2 ounces creamed coconut

1 tablespoon coconut oil + extra to fry

Instructions

1. Place a soup pot over medium heat. Add coconut oil. When the oil melts, add onions and sauté until translucent.

2. Stir in bell pepper and garlic and sauté until fragrant.

3. Stir in broccoli, cauliflower, water and bouillon.

4. Cook until the vegetables are tender. Add curry paste and creamed coconut and mix well.

5. Lower heat and let it simmer.

6. Meanwhile, place a small deep pan with a little coconut oil. When the oil is heated, add tofu cubes and cook until crisp and golden brown in color.

7. Ladle soup into the bowls. Top with tofu cubes and serve.

ROASTED TOMATO SOUP

Makes 3 (¾ cup each) servings

Ingredients

5 medium Roma tomatoes, cubed

2 cloves garlic, minced

2 tablespoons heavy cream

Sea salt to taste

Pepper to taste

½ tablespoon olive oil

2-3 tablespoons water

A handful fresh basil, minced

Instructions

1. Place a sheet of aluminum foil on a baking sheet. Grease it with a little cooking spray.

2. Add tomatoes into a bowl. Add garlic and oil and toss well. Spread it on the prepared baking sheet.

3. Roast in a preheated oven at 400°F for 20-25 or until the skin has blisters on it and is lightly charred.

4. Remove from the oven and cool for a while. Transfer the tomatoes into a blender along with the juices and garlic. Blend until smooth.

5. Transfer into a soup pot. Place the pot over medium heat. Add salt, pepper and water and stir. Bring to the boil.

6. Lower heat and simmer for 5-8 minutes.

7. Add cream and basil. Stir and turn off heat.

8. Ladle into soup bowls and serve.

CHICKEN FAJITA SOUP

Makes 4 servings

Ingredients

1lb chicken breast, skinless, boneless

1 small onion, chopped

2 cloves garlic, minced

3 ounces cream cheese

2 cups chicken broth, divided

3 teaspoons taco seasoning

Pepper to taste

Salt to taste

½ tablespoon butter

To serve:

Shredded cheese

Sour crea

Fresh cilantro

Instructions

1. Add chicken into a saucepan. Sprinkle salt and pepper over it. Place saucepan over medium low heat and cook until tender. (You can also cook in a slow cooker).

2. When chicken is cooked, shred chicken with a pair of forks. Retain the cooked broth. Set aside.

3. Place a large saucepan over medium heat. Add butter. When butter melts, add onion and garlic and sauté until translucent.

4. Stir in the cream cheese. Mash it with the back of a spoon so that it is well combined.

5. Add remaining broth, cooked broth, tomatoes, taco seasoning and heavy cream.

6. Cook without covering for 15 minutes.

7. Add chicken, salt and pepper. Cover and cook for 7-8 minutes.

8. Ladle into soup bowls and serve garnished with cilantro, sour cream and cheese.

HIGH FAT HAMBURGER SOUP

Makes 3 servings

Ingredients

1 medium onion, chopped

1 medium yellow bell pepper, sliced

2 cups beef stock with fat

10 Brussels sprouts, halved

2 tablespoons red palm oil, melted

Freshly ground pepper to taste

Himalayan rock salt to taste

2 cloves garlic, minced

½ lb grass fed regular ground beef

3 stalks celery, chopped

1 cup whole tomatoes

1 bay leaf

Instructions

1. Place mushrooms, onion, bell pepper and Brussels sprouts on a baking sheet.

2. Drizzle oil over it. Sprinkle salt and pepper and toss.

3. Roast in a preheated oven at 350° F for 25-30 minutes. Remove from the oven and set aside.

4. Place a soup pot over medium heat. Add beef and sauté until brown. Add celery and garlic and sauté for a couple of minutes. Add rest of the ingredients and stir.

5. Bring to the boil. Lower heat and cover with a lid. Simmer for 15-20 minutes.

6. Add the roasted vegetables and heat thoroughly. Garnish with parsley.

7. Ladle into soup bowls and serve.

1/8 teaspoon cayenne pepper or chili powder

5 mushrooms, chopped

½ tablespoon tomato paste

½ teaspoon dried oregano

2 tablespoons fresh parsley, chopped

CHAPTER EIGHT

KETO SMOOTHIE RECIPES

AVOCADO AND COCONUT WATER SMOOTHIE

Makes 2 servings

Ingredients

1 medium avocado, peeled, pitted, chopped

1 cup coconut milk or ½ cup heavy whipping cream along with ½ cup water

1 teaspoon vanilla powder or vanilla extract

4 tablespoons erythritol or Stevia drops to taste

1 cup fresh spinach

1-1 ½ cups water

Ice cubes, as required

2 tablespoons MCT oil or extra virgin coconut oil

2 teaspoons matcha powder (optional)

Instructions

1. Add all the ingredients into a blender and blend until smooth.

2. Pour into tall glasses and serve.

BUTTER SMOOTHIE

Makes 2 servings

Ingredients

4 teaspoons cocoa powder

2 cups almond milk or coconut milk

1 cup almond butter

Swerve sweetener to taste

Instructions

1. Collect all the ingredients and add into the blender. Blend for 30-40 seconds or until smooth.

2. Pour into tall glasses and serve with crushed ice.

SPICY GREEN SMOOTHIE

Makes 2 servings

Ingredients

1 cup spinach leaves

¼ cup English cucumber

¼ cup red bell pepper

1 clove garlic, peeled

½ tablespoon lemon juice

Freshly ground pepper to taste

A pinch chili powders

½ avocado, peeled, pitted, chopped

1 small green onion, chopped

¼ cup vegetable broth

½ tablespoon soy seasoning

Instructions

1. Collect all the ingredients and add into the blender. Blend for 30-40 seconds or until smooth.

2. Pour into tall glasses and serve with crushed ice.

STRAWBERRY HEMP SEED SMOOTHIE

Makes 4 servings

Ingredients

2 cups milk of your choice

2 cups frozen strawberries

1 cup frozen raspberries

½ cup frozen blackberries

½ cup frozen blueberries

½ cup hemp seeds

2 cups vanilla yogurt

2 teaspoons vanilla extract

Instructions

1. Collect all the ingredients and add into the blender. Blend for 30-40 seconds or until smooth.

2. Pour into tall glasses and serve with crushed ice.

STRAWBERRY RHUBARB SMOOTHIE

Makes 2 servings

Ingredients

8 strawberries

2 large eggs

4 medium rhubarb stalks

1 cup almond milk

2 ounces almonds or 4 tablespoons almond butter

4 tablespoons full fat cream or coconut milk

1 teaspoon pure vanilla bean extract

2 teaspoons fresh ginger root, grated

10-12 drops liquid Stevia or to taste

Instructions

1. Add strawberries, eggs, rhubarb stalks, almond milk, almonds, cream, vanilla extract, ginger and Stevia into a blender until smooth.

2. Pour into tall glasses and serve with crushed ice.

GREEN DEVIL

Makes 4 servings

Ingredients

3 cups coconut water

4 tablespoons ground flax seed

1 cup coconut milk

Juice of 2 lemons

1 avocado, peeled, pitted, chopped

6 stalks celery, chopped

12 romaine lettuce leaves, chopped

8 large kale leaves, discard hard stems and ribs

1 cup spinach leaves, chopped

Instructions

1. Collect all the ingredients and add into the blender. Blend for 30-40 seconds or until smooth.

2. Pour into tall glasses and serve with crushed ice.

PUMPKIN SPICE LATTE SMOOTHIE

Makes 4 servings

Ingredients

2 cups almond milk or any other milk of your choice, unsweetened

1 cup canned pumpkin

4 teaspoons pumpkin pie spice

Stevia drops to taste

½ cup ice cubes

4 teaspoons instant coffee granules

2 tablespoons hemp seeds

Instructions

1. Collect all the ingredients and add into the blender. Blend for 30-40 seconds or until smooth.

2. Pour into tall glasses and serve.

VERY BERRY SMOOTHIE

Makes 4 servings

Ingredients

2 ½ cups frozen raspberries

7-8 strawberries, hulled, sliced

4 teaspoons fresh ginger, grated

1 ½ cups almond milk, unsweetened or rice milk

2 teaspoons ground flaxseeds

Stevia drops to taste

1 ½ tablespoons lemon juice

Instructions

1. Collect all the ingredients and add into the blender. Blend for 30-40 seconds or until smooth.

2. Pour into tall glasses and serve.

VEGETABLE SMOOTHIE

Makes 2 servings

Ingredients

2 cups spinach or kale or any other dark leafy greens of your choice

1 red bell pepper, chopped

4 tomatoes, chopped

2 cloves garlic, peeled

2 stalks celery, chopped

1 small red onion, chopped

Zest of 1 lime, grated

½ cup chopped cilantro

2 cups water

1 jalapeño pepper, chopped, deseed if desired

2-3 inches fresh turmeric, sliced or ½ teaspoon ground turmeric powder

1 cup ice cubes or as required

Instructions

1. Collect all the ingredients and add into the blender. Blend for 30-40 seconds or until smooth.

2. Pour into tall glasses and serve.

MCKETO STRAWBERRY MILKSHAKE

Makes 2 servings

Ingredients

2 cups coconut milk, from carton

4 tablespoons sugar free strawberry syrup

½ teaspoon xanthan gum

½ cup heavy cream

2 tablespoons MCT oil

Ice cubes, as required

Instructions

1. Collect all the ingredients and add into the blender. Blend for 30-40 seconds or until smooth.

2. Pour into tall glasses and serve.

SPICY TOMATO SMOOTHIE

Makes 2 servings

Ingredients

1 cup tomatoes

1 avocado, peeled, pitted, chopped

1 small cucumber, peel if desired, chopped

2/3 cup chopped spinach

Juice of a lemon

2 teaspoons hot sauce

Instructions

1. Collect all the ingredients and add into the blender. Blend for 30-40 seconds or until smooth.

2. Pour into tall glasses and serve with crushed ice.

STRAWBERRIES 'N' CREAM SMOOTHIE BOWL

Makes 2 servings

Ingredients

2 cups frozen strawberries

½ cup almond milk, unsweetened

½ teaspoon pure vanilla extract

10 strawberries, sliced + extra to top

¼ cup almonds, sliced

2 teaspoons chia seeds

1 cup full fat Greek yogurt

2 tablespoons sugar-free maple syrup + extra to drizzle

½ cup blueberries

2 tablespoons pumpkin seeds

Instructions

1. Add strawberries, yogurt, vanilla and sugar-free maple syrup into a blender.
2. Blend for 30-40 seconds or until smooth.
3. Pour into 2 bowls.
4. Sprinkle chia seeds, pumpkin seeds and almonds on top.
5. Place strawberry slices and blueberries on top.
6. Drizzle some sugar-free maple syrup and yogurt if desired.
7. Serve.

EGG CREAM SMOOTHIE

Makes 2 servings

Ingredients

4 eggs

½ cup heavy cream

Ice cubes, as required

¼ cup cream cheese

2 tablespoons sugar-free vanilla syrup

Instructions

1. Crack the eggs into a blender. Add rest of the ingredients.

2. Blend until smooth.

3. Pour into glasses and serve with crushed ice.

SALTED CARAMEL CASHEW SMOOTHIE

Makes 2 servings

Ingredients

2 cups cashew milk, unsweetened

Ice cubes, as required

Pumpkin pie spice, to sprinkle

4 tablespoons sugar-free salted caramel syrup

1/3 cup heavy cream

Instructions

1. Collect all the ingredients and add into the blender. Blend for 30-40 seconds or until smooth.

2. Pour into glasses.

3. Sprinkle pumpkin pie spice on top and serve.

RASPBERRY AND CHOCOLATE CHEESECAKE SMOOTHIE

Makes 2 servings

Ingredients

½ cup full fat cream cheese or creamed coconut milk

2/3 cup raspberries, fresh or frozen

1 cup water

Stevia drops to taste (optional)

½ cup heavy whipping cream or coconut milk

2 tablespoons cacao powder, unsweetened

2 tablespoons MCT oil or extra virgin coconut oil

Instructions

1. Collect all the ingredients and add into the blender. Blend for 30-40 seconds or until smooth.

2. Pour into glasses and serve with ice if desired.

CINNAMON SMOOTHIE

Makes 2 servings

Ingredients

2 ½ cups almond milk

1 ½ teaspoons cinnamon powder

4 tablespoons vanilla protein powder

2 teaspoons flax meal

2 teaspoons chia seeds

½ teaspoon vanilla extract

Stevia drops to taste or erythritol to taste

Ice as required

Instructions

1. Collect all the ingredients and add into the blender. Blend for 30-40 seconds or until smooth.

CHAPTER NINE

KETO APPETIZER RECIPES

CHEESY ASPARAGUS

Makes 2 servings

Ingredients

½ lb asparagus, trimmed

2 teaspoons Italian seasoning, divided or to taste

¼ cup Parmesan cheese, shredded

¼ cup mozzarella cheese, shredded

2 teaspoons olive oil

Sea salt to taste

Pepper to taste

Instructions

1. Place parchment paper or foil on a baking sheet. Spray with a little cooking spray.

2. Place asparagus on the baking sheet. Drizzle oil. Sprinkle 1 teaspoon Italian seasoning, salt and pepper. Toss well.

3. Roast in a preheated oven at 400° F for about 7-9 minutes.

4. Add mozzarella cheese and Parmesan cheese into a bowl and mix. Sprinkle over the asparagus. Sprinkle 1 teaspoon Italian seasoning.

5. Broil for 5-6 minutes or until the cheese melts and is golden brown at spots.

CRISPY SALT AND PEPPER SPICED TOFU

Makes 6-8 servings

Ingredients

28 ounces extra firm tofu, pressed of excess moisture, chopped into 1 inch cubes

Freshly cracked black pepper to taste

Salt to taste

4 tablespoons almond meal

Vegetable oil for frying as required

2 teaspoons Chinese 5 spice powder

2 teaspoons dried chili flakes

Salt to taste

Pepper powder taste

Soy sauce to taste

To garnish:

Celery leaves, chopped

Instructions

1. Add tofu into a bowl. Drizzle soy and toss well.
2. Mix together almond meal, chili flakes, 5 spice powder, salt and pepper in a bowl and sprinkle over the tofu. Toss until all the pieces are coated.
3. Place a deep pan over low heat and pour some oil.
4. Once the oil is heated, fry the tofu pieces in batches until crisp and golden brown. Stir occasionally.
5. Remove with a slotted spoon and place over paper towels.
6. Serve with a dip of your choice.

2 spring onions, thinly sliced

1 red onion, thinly sliced

AVOCADO TUNA MELT BITES

Makes 8 (3 bites per serving)

Ingredients

2 cans (10 ounces each) tuna, drained

2 medium avocadoes, peeled, pitted, cubed

2/3 cup almond flour + extra to dredge

Pepper to taste

Salt to taste

½ teaspoon onion powder

1 teaspoon garlic powder

1 cup coconut oil to deep fry

Instructions

1. Add all the ingredients except coconut oil and avocado into a bowl and mix well.

2. Add avocado and mix well. Divide into 24 equal portions and shape into balls.

3. Place some almond flour in a shallow bowl. Dredge the balls in the flour.

4. Place a small, deep pan over medium heat. Add oil and heat. When the oil is sufficiently hot but not smoking, add the balls, 3-4 at a time and fry until brown.

5. Remove with a slotted spoon and place on a plate lined with paper towels. Repeat with the remaining balls.

6. Serve with a keto-friendly dip of your choice.

FISH FINGERS

Makes 6 servings

Ingredients

6 ounces white fish, rinsed, cut into fingers

½ teaspoon garlic powder

1 egg, beaten

2 tablespoons coconut flour

1 tablespoons seasoned salt or to taste

1 teaspoon garlic powder

Pepper powder to taste

½ cup coconut oil

Instructions

1. Add coconut flour, seasoned salt, garlic powder and pepper powder into a bowl.

2. First dip the fish fingers in the egg and then roll in the coconut mixture and set aside on a plate.

3. Add ¼ cup oil to a small, deep pan and place over medium heat.

4. Fry the fish fingers in batches until brown.

5. Serve with any keto friendly dip of your choice.

INSTANT POT SHRIMP IN GARLIC SAUCE

Makes 4 servings

Ingredients

1 lb extra-large shrimp, peeled, deveined

1 green onion, chopped

2 tablespoons extra virgin olive oil

3 cloves garlic, minced

¼ teaspoon red pepper flakes

½ teaspoon smoked paprika

2 teaspoons fresh parsley minced to garnish

Salt to taste

Pepper to taste

Instructions

1. Add all the ingredients except shrimp and parsley into the instant pot.

2. Close the lid. Press 'Slow cook' button and set the timer for 20 minutes.

3. Add shrimp and cook for 10 more minutes or until the shrimp turns opaque.

4. Transfer into a serving dish. Garnish with parsley and serve warm.

CAULIFLOWER CHEESE & ONION CROQUETTES

Makes 2 (makes 6 croquettes servings)

Ingredients

1 small cauliflower, chopped into florets

1 teaspoon garlic powder

¼ cup cheddar cheese, grated

¼ teaspoon salt

1 tablespoon olive oil

½ cup Parmesan cheese, grated

2 spring onions, finely chopped

¼ teaspoon Dijon mustard

¼ teaspoon pepper

Instructions

1. Place a saucepan over medium heat. Add cauliflower and cover with water. When it begins to boil, lower heat and cover with a lid.

2. Simmer until tender. Drain and squeeze out excess water from the cauliflower.

3. Add cauliflower into a bowl and mash well.

4. Add spring onions, cheddar cheese, Parmesan cheese, mustard, garlic powder, salt and pepper. Mix well.

5. Divide the mixture into 6 equal portions and shape into croquettes.

6. Place a sheet of parchment paper on a plate. Place croquettes on it. Chill for 30-40 minutes.

7. Place a nonstick pan over medium heat. Add oil. When the oil is heated, place croquettes and cook until golden brown. Flip sides and cook the other side too.

8. Cook in batches if required.

ZUCCHINI PATTIES

Makes 12 servings

Ingredients

1 lb zucchini, grated

1 large handful fresh herbs (mixture of mint, parsley and dill)

½ cup feta cheese, crumbled

½ teaspoon fine grain sea salt

4 teaspoons olive oil, divided

1 large egg

½ cup almond meal

½ teaspoon ground cumin

Pepper to taste

Salt to taste

Instructions

1. Sprinkle salt over the zucchini and place in a colander. Let it drain for 30-60 minutes.

2. Squeeze the zucchini of excess moisture.

3. Add egg into a large bowl and beat well. Add zucchini, mixed herbs, feta cheese, almond meal, cumin, salt and pepper. Mix well.

4. Place the bowl in the refrigerator for 20-30 minutes.

5. Remove the bowl from the refrigerator. If you find that the mixture is very wet, add a little more of almond meal and mix well.

6. Divide the mixture into 12 equal portions and shape into patties.

7. Place a nonstick pan over medium heat. Add 2 teaspoons oil. When the oil is heated, place a few patties on it. Cook until the underside is golden brown. Flip sides and cook the other side too. Remove with a slotted spoon and place on a plate that is lined with paper towels.

8. Repeat the above step with the remaining patties. Make them in 2-3 batches.

9. Serve.

SMOKED PAPRIKA ZUCCHINI CHIPS

Makes 7-8 servings

Ingredients

3 medium zucchinis

Salt to taste

Olive oil cooking spray

3 -4 teaspoons smoked paprika

2 teaspoons onion powder

Pepper powder to taste

Instructions

1. Cut the zucchini into 1/8th inch thick slices, crosswise with a mandolin slicer or a sharp knife.

2. Place the zucchini on a sieve in layers sprinkled with salt and pepper. Keep aside for an hour. Some moisture content of the zucchini will drain out.

3. Pat dry the zucchini slices with a paper towel and place on a greased baking tray.

4. Brush the top of the slices with oil. Sprinkle onion powder, paprika and pepper.

5. Bake in a preheated oven at 250º F for 45 minutes. Rotate the baking tray 2-3 times while baking.

6. Turn off the oven and let the chips remain inside for an hour so that it remains crispy.

7. Transfer into an airtight container.

BACON WRAPPED CHEESE STICKS

Makes 2 servings

Ingredients

6 strips partially cooked bacon

3 pieces string cheese, halved lengthwise

Oil to fry, as required

Instructions

1. Take one piece of string cheese and wrap it with 1 bacon strip. Place on a tray.

2. Repeat the same with the remaining pieces of cheese and bacon slices.

3. Place tray in the freezer for an hour.

4. Place a small deep pan over medium heat. Pour enough oil to cover the bottom of the pan by about ½ inch.

5. When the oil heats to 350° F, drop a few of the bacon wrapped cheese in the pan.

6. Fry until golden brown on all the sides.

7. Remove with a slotted spoon and place on a plate lined with paper towels for a few minutes before serving.

8. Repeat with the remaining wrapped pieces.

9. Serve with a keto friendly dip of your choice.

CHILI AND ROSEMARY ROASTED NUTS

Makes 8 servings

Ingredients

9 ounces mixed nuts of your choice (like cashew, almonds and pistachio)

1 teaspoon chili powder or to taste

2 teaspoons avocado oil

¼ teaspoon ground cumin

½ tablespoon fresh rosemary, chopped

1 tablespoon lemon juice

Instructions

1. Add all the ingredients into a bowl and stir until the nuts are well coated.

2. Place nuts on a rimmed baking sheet that is lined with parchment paper.

3. Roast in a preheated oven at 325° F for 12-15 minutes. Stir the nuts every 4-5 minutes until the nuts are ready. Keep a watch on the nuts after 8 minutes as they can get burnt easily.

4. Remove the baking sheet from the oven and cool completely.

5. Store in an airtight container until use.

AVOCADO BALLS

Makes 12 servings

Ingredients

1 large avocado, peeled, pitted, chopped

4 cloves garlic, crushed

1 small white onion, chopped

Freshly ground black or cayenne pepper

¼ cup fresh cilantro, chopped

½ cup ghee or butter, at room temperature

2 small chili peppers, finely chopped

2 tablespoons fresh lime juice

½ teaspoon salt or to taste

8 large slices bacon

Instructions

1. Place a nonstick pan over medium heat. Add bacon and cook until crisp.

2. Remove with a slotted spoon and place on a place that is lined with paper towels. When cool enough to handle, crumble and set aside. Retain the bacon fat.

3. Add all the ingredients except onions into a bowl. Mash well.

4. Add onion and mix until well combined. Add the retained bacon fat and mix again.

5. Cover and chill for 30-40 minutes.

6. Divide the mixture into 12 equal portions and shape into balls.

7. Dredge the balls in crumbled bacon and place on a serving platter. Refrigerate for a while and serve.

ITALIAN STUFFED MUSHROOMS

Makes 10 (4 each) servings

Ingredients

2 lbs crimini mushrooms (about 40)

8 large clove garlic, minced

1 cup parmesan cheese, grated

Sea salt to taste

Pepper to taste

2 lbs mild Italian sausage

16 ounces cream cheese, softened

A handful sprigs Italian flat leaf parsley, chopped

Instructions

1. Remove the stems of the mushrooms carefully and finely chop them. Set the caps aside.

2. Place a skillet over medium -high heat. Add Italian sausage, finely chopped mushroom and garlic. Cook until sausage turns brown. Turn off the heat. When it cools completely, Transfer into a bowl.

3. Add cream cheese, ½ cup Parmesan cheese, salt, pepper and parsley into the bowl of sausage and mix well. Taste and adjust the seasoning if required.

4. Fill some of the mixture into the mushroom caps, in a mound.

5. Place the mushroom caps on a baking sheet.

6. Place rack in the center of the oven.

7. Bake in a preheated oven at 350°F for about 15-20 minutes.

8. Sprinkle remaining cheese over the mushrooms and broil for a couple of minutes until cheese melts.

9. Remove from the oven and cool for 8-10 minutes before serving.

CRUSTY CHEDDAR

Makes 4 servings

Ingredients

4 slices cheddar cheese (1.8 ounces each)

2 teaspoons flaxseed, ground

2 teaspoons hemp nuts

Salt to taste

Pepper powder to taste

2 eggs

2 teaspoons almond flour

2 tablespoons olive oil

Instructions

1. Add eggs, salt, and pepper into a bowl and whisk well.

2. Mix together in a shallow bowl, flaxseed, almond flour, and hemp nuts.

3. Place a nonstick frying pan over medium heat. Add about ½ tablespoon of oil.

4. Dip a cheddar slice in the egg mixture. Shake to drop off excess egg. Dredge the cheddar slice in the flaxseed mixture.

5. Place the cheddar slice in the pan and cook on both the sides until golden brown.

6. Repeat steps 3 – 5 with the remaining cheddar slices.

7. Serve hot.

PISTACHIO CRUSTED SUN-DRIED TOMATO GOAT CHEESE BALLS

Makes 7 (2 balls each) servings

Ingredients

2 packages (4 ounce each) sundried tomato goat cheese

Salt to taste

1 cup pistachios, shelled, crush them with a rolling pin or a mortar and pestle

Instructions

1. Mix together salt and pistachio in a bowl.

2. Mash the goat cheese in a bowl. Divide the cheese into 14 equal portions and shape into small balls with your hands.

3. Roll the balls in the pistachio mixture and serve.

COCONUT TORTILLAS

Makes 18-20 servings

Ingredients

1 cup coconut flour

2 ½ cups almond milk, unsweetened

10 large eggs

1 teaspoon sea salt

Cooking spray

Instructions

1. Add all the ingredients into a bowl. Whisk well. Set aside for 5 minutes. The batter should pour easily and should be runny. Add more milk or eggs in equal quantities if required.

2. Place a small skillet or pan over medium heat. Spray with cooking spray. Pour ¼ cup of the prepared batter on the skillet. Swirl the pan so that the batter spreads evenly.

3. Cover the pan with a lid. Cook until the edges begin to get golden brown. Flip sides. Cover and cook until done. Remove and place on a plate.

4. Repeat with the remaining batter to make remaining tortillas.

KALE STUFFED PORTOBELLO MUSHROOMS

Makes 8 servings

Ingredients

16 large Portobello mushrooms, discard stem and gills

16 slices cheese of your choice

12 ounces fresh kale, discard hard ribs and stems

4 tablespoons extra virgin olive oil

Instructions

1. Grease a baking sheet with cooking spray. Place mushrooms on the baking sheet. Drizzle oil over the mushrooms.

2. Bake in a preheated oven at 375° F for 10 minutes. Remove the baking sheet from the oven. Place kale in the mushroom caps. Place cheese slice over the kale.

3. Bake for 2-3 minutes and serve.

SALMON FAT BOMBS

Makes 12 servings

Ingredients

1 cup full fat cream cheese

1 package smoked salmon

¼ cup fresh dill, chopped or 2 teaspoons dried dill + extra to garnish

2/3 cup butter

2 tablespoons fresh lemon juice

Salt to taste, preferably Himalayan pink salt

Instructions

1. Add butter, cream cheese and smoked salmon into the food processor bowl. Pulse until well combined.

2. Add lemon juice and dill and process until well combined. Transfer into a bowl.

3. Divide the mixture 12 equal portions and shape into balls (or add into molds of your choice).

4. Place the balls on a baking tray that is lined with parchment paper (place molds in the refrigerator if using molds). Sprinkle dill on top. Press lightly. Chill until firm.

5. Store in an airtight container in the refrigerator until use. It can last for a week.

KALE AND BACON CHIPS

Makes 10 servings

Ingredients

2 bunches kale, discard hard stems and ribs, torn (about 10 cups)

4 tablespoons butter

1 teaspoon garlic powder

½ cup bacon grease

1-2 teaspoons salt or to taste

Instructions

1. Line a baking sheet with parchment paper and set aside.

2. Dry the kale leaves thoroughly.

3. Add butter and bacon grease into a small pan. Place the pan over low heat. Turn off the heat when the mixture melts.

4. Add salt and mix well. Add kale and toss well until kale is well coated.

5. Spread the leaves on the prepared baking sheet in a single layer. Sprinkle garlic powder on it.

6. Bake in a preheated oven at 300° F for 25 minutes or until crisp and dark green in color. Remove the baking sheet from the oven. Cool completely. Bake in batches if necessary.

7. Serve immediately or store in an airtight container. It can last for 2 days.

CHOCOLATE PEANUT BUTTER FAT BOMB

Makes 20-25 servings

Ingredients

½ cup peanut butter, unsweetened

2 ounces baking chocolate, unsweetened

1 teaspoon vanilla Stevia drops

½ cup coconut oil

2 tablespoons cocoa

Instructions

1. Add all the ingredients except Stevia into a microwave safe bowl. Microwave on high for 1-2 minutes or until it melts completely. Stir every 20 seconds after the initial 40 seconds.

2. Add Stevia drops. Stir and pour into 20-25 small silicone molds or ice cube trays.

3. Place in the freezer until it sets.

4. Remove from the molds and transfer into a freezer safe container. Freeze until use.

ANTIPASTO KEBABS

Makes 6 (2 skewers each) servings

Ingredients

12 baby heirloom tomatoes

12 Spanish queen green olives

12 fresh mozzarella balls

12 slices salami

12 kalamata olives

12 pepperoncini's

12 cubes sharp cheddar cheese

12 pepperoni slices

12 prosciutto slices

12 roasted red peppers

12 marinated mushrooms

Instructions

1. Insert one of each of the ingredient into each of 12 skewers.
2. Serve.

CHAPTER TEN

KETO SALAD RECIPES

KETO CRACK SLAW

Makes 4 servings

Ingredients

8 cups green cabbage, shredded

2 teaspoons chili paste or sriracha sauce

4 tablespoons tamari or liquid aminos

4 cloves garlic

1 cup macadamia nuts, chopped

2 teaspoons vinegar

2 tablespoons sesame oil

Sesame seeds to garnish

1 green onion, thinly sliced, to garnish

Instructions

1. Add cabbage, chili paste, tamari, garlic, and vinegar and sesame oil into a bowl and toss well. Cover and set aside for 5-7 minutes.

2. Place a wok or skillet over medium high heat. Add the cabbage mixture into the wok.

3. Sauté for 3-4 minutes. Add macadamia nuts and sauté for 5-7 minutes.

4. Garnish with sesame seeds and green onion and serve.

SWEET N SPICY SALAD

Makes 8 servings

Ingredients

6 cups fresh spinach leaves

10 slices turkey bacon

1 cup red bell pepper, chopped

1 cup orange bell pepper, chopped

1 cup green bell pepper, chopped

1 cup yellow bell pepper, chopped

6 jalapeno peppers, chopped

1 cup onions, chopped

2 cups alfalfa sprouts

1 cup Cabot habanero cheddar, sliced

½ cup Italian salad dressing

Instructions

1. Place a nonstick pan over medium heat. Add the bacon slices and cook on both the sides until brown. Remove bacon with a slotted spoon. When cool enough to handle, crumble the bacon.

2. Add rest of the ingredients to a large bowl. Toss well.

3. Top with bacon and serve.

MEDITERRANEAN CHOPPED SALAD

Makes 2 servings

Ingredients

1 medium tomato, deseeded, chopped

2 scallions, chopped

2 tablespoons kalamata olives pitted, coarsely chopped

1 small seedless cucumber, chopped

A handful fresh parsley, chopped

1 tablespoon extra-virgin olive oil

Salt to taste

½ tablespoon white wine vinegar

Freshly ground pepper to taste

Instructions

1. Add all the ingredients into a bowl and toss well.
2. Serve right away.

BACON BLUE ZOODLE SALAD

Makes 4 servings

Ingredients

8 cups zucchini noodles

2 cups fresh broccoli florets

1 cup bacon

2 cups fresh spinach

2/3 cup blue cheese, crumbled

2/3 cup thick or chunky bleu cheese dressing

Freshly cracked pepper to taste

Instructions

1. Make noodles of the zucchini using a spiralizer or a julienne peeler.

2. Place a nonstick pan over medium heat. Add bacon. Sauté until crisp.

3. Remove bacon with a slotted spoon. When cool enough to handle, crumble the bacon.

4. Add rest of the ingredients of the salad into a bowl. Pour dressing on top and toss well.

5. Serve immediately.

HEALTHY COBB SALAD

Makes 2 servings

Ingredients

For garlic and herb vinaigrette dressing:

2 tablespoons olive oil

2 tablespoon apple cider vinegar

2 teaspoons lemon juice

2 teaspoons Dijon mustard

½ teaspoon garlic, minced

Salt to taste

Pepper to taste

2 tablespoons finely minced fresh herbs of your choice

For the salad:

5 slices bacon

2 large green onions, chopped

4 medium large radishes, sliced

Instructions

1. To make salad dressing: Add olive oil, apple cider vinegar, lemon juice, Dijon mustard, garlic, salt, pepper and herbs into a small jar.

2. Fasten the lid. Shake the jar vigorously until well combined. Set aside for a while for the flavors to set in. Use as much as vinaigrette as required. The remaining can be used in some other recipe or refrigerated for a couple of days and used later.

3. Place a nonstick skillet over medium heat. Add bacon and sauté for 3-5 minutes until brown and crisp.

4. Remove with a slotted spoon and place on a plate lined with layers of paper towels. When cool enough to handle, crumble and set aside.

5. Place lettuce at the bottom of the serving bowl. Place the rest of the ingredients over the lettuce next to each other in rows i.e. a row of tomatoes, next a row of avocado slices, similarly rows of blue cheese, bell peppers, green onion, bacon and eggs.

6. Shake the dressing well before use and pour as much as required over the salad.

7. Serve.

1 large green bell pepper, deseeded, sliced

1 large red bell pepper, deseeded, sliced

4 cherry tomatoes, halved (optional)

2 ounces blue cheese, crumbled

2 hard- boiled eggs, shelled, sliced

4 cups romaine lettuce, coarsely chopped

1 medium avocado, peeled, pitted, diced

4 ounces grilled chicken

EASY KETO SLAW

Makes 3 servings

Ingredients

2 1/2 ounces red cabbage, thinly sliced

4 1/2 ounces green or white cabbage, thinly sliced

2 ounces fennel bulb, thinly sliced

1 1/2 ounces celeriac, grated

For Russian dressing:

3 tablespoon mayonnaise

½ tablespoon Sriracha chili sauce

½ teaspoon horseradish, freshly grated

1 tablespoon fresh parsley, finely chopped

1 tablespoon lemon juice

1 tablespoon chives, finely chopped

Instructions

1. Add all the ingredients of dressing into a bowl and mix well.

2. Add all the vegetables into a bowl and toss well. Pour dressing on top. Fold gently and serve.

1 small pickled cucumber

1 tablespoon sour cream or coconut milk

Freshly ground pepper to taste

Salt to taste

LEMON BLUEBERRY CHICKEN SALAD

Makes 2 servings

Ingredients

20 blueberries

2 large bags salad leaves (about 4.5 ounces each)

4 teaspoons fresh lemon juice

4 tablespoons coconut oil

1 small onion, sliced

4 tablespoons olive oil

1 lb chicken breast, boneless, skinless, chopped into bite size pieces

Salt to taste

Pepper to taste

Instructions

1. Place a skillet over medium heat. Add coconut oil. When oil melts, add chicken and cook until done.

2. Add salt and pepper and sauté for a minute.

3. Transfer into a serving bowl. Add blueberries, onion, olive oil, salad leaves and lemon juice and toss well.

4. Divide into individual serving bowls and serve.

LOBSTER ROLL SALAD

Makes 2 servings

Ingredients

For lobster salad:

1 cup lobster meat, chopped into bite size pieces

¼ cup sugar free mayonnaise

¾ cup cauliflower flowerets, cooked, chilled

1 teaspoon fresh tarragon leaves, chopped

To serve:

4 fresh romaine lettuce leaves

¼ cup bacon, cooked, chopped

1 small tomato, chopped

Instructions

1. To make salad: Add all the ingredients of lobster salad into a bowl and fold gently.

2. To serve: Place the lettuce leaves on a serving platter. Divide and place the salad on the leaves. Top with tomatoes and bacon.

3. Roll and serve at room temperature or chilled.

GRILLED HALLOUMI SALAD

Makes 2 servings

Ingredients

6 ounces halloumi cheese, cut into 1/3 inch thick slices

10 grape tomatoes, halved

1 ounce walnuts, chopped

Balsamic vinegar to drizzle

2 cucumbers, chopped

2 cups baby arugula

Olive oil, to drizzle

Salt to taste

Instructions

1. Place a grill pan over medium heat. Let it preheat for a few minutes.

2. Place the halloumi slices over it. Grill for 3-5 minutes. Flip sides and grill the other side.

3. Add tomatoes, walnuts, cucumber and arugula into a bowl and toss well.

4. Place grilled halloumi over it. Season with salt.

5. Drizzle oil and vinegar and serve.

LOADED CHICKEN SALAD

Makes 2 servings

Ingredients

1 chicken breast half (about 5.75 -6 ounces), boneless

1/8 teaspoon Himalayan salt

½ avocado, peeled, pitted, chopped

1 medium tomato, chopped

1 small red onion, sliced

10 fresh basil leaves, stack them up and thinly slice

1 3/4 ounces mozzarella balls

½ jar artichoke hearts (from a 6 ounces jar)

3 asparagus, trimmed, halved

2 cups baby spinach

½ tablespoon extra-virgin olive oil

Pepper to taste

Instructions

1. Split the chicken breast halve into 2, lengthwise. Season with salt and pepper.

2. Place a skillet over medium heat. Add oil and heat. Add chicken and cook for 3 minutes or until the underside is golden brown. Flip sides and cook the other side until golden brown.

3. Place asparagus next to the chicken and cook until soft. Remove chicken and place on your cutting board.

4. When cool enough to handle, slice the chicken.

5. Meanwhile make the dressing as follows: Whisk together all the ingredients of dressing in a bowl.

6. Divide spinach among 2 serving plates. Lay chicken slices over it along with asparagus and rest of the salad ingredients. Drizzle the dressing on top and serve.

For dressing:

1 tablespoon extra-virgin olive oil

½ teaspoon Dijon mustard

A pinch Himalayan salt

2 teaspoons balsamic vinegar

1 small clove garlic, minced

A pinch pepper

BALSAMIC FLAT IRON STEAK SALAD

Makes 2 servings

Ingredients

¾ lb flat iron steak, cut into ½ inch thick slices

1 ½ tablespoons avocado oil or olive oil

2 ounces crimini mushrooms, sliced

1 medium head romaine lettuce, chopped

½ red bell pepper, sliced

½ orange bell pepper, sliced

½ teaspoon garlic salt

½ teaspoon Italian seasoning

½ teaspoon onion powder

½ teaspoon red pepper flakes

2 tablespoons balsamic vinegar

3 ounces sweet onion, sliced

Instructions

1. Toss together meat and vinegar in a bowl. Set aside.

2. Place a skillet over medium low heat. Add oil and heat. Add mushrooms, garlic, salt, pepper and onion and sauté until golden brown. It may take 15-20 minutes.

3. Add romaine, bell peppers, avocado and sun dried tomatoes into a bowl.

4. Place meat strips in a single layer in a broiling pan. Do not overlap.

5. Mix together, garlic salt, seasoning, onion powder ad red pepper flakes in a bowl. Sprinkle it over the meat.

6. Place the pan on the top rack and broil for 4-5 minutes until medium rare.

7. Remove from the oven.

8. To assemble: Divide the salad on individual plates. Place mushroom mixture on it. Place flat iron strips and serve.

1 clove garlic, minced

1 small avocado, peeled, pitted, sliced

1 1/2 ounces sun dried tomatoes

CHEESEBURGER SALAD

Makes 3 servings

Ingredients

For burger crumble:

½ lb extra lean ground beef

1 ½ tablespoons Worcestershire sauce

Freshly ground pepper to taste

½ cup yellow onion, diced

¼ teaspoon seasoning salt or to taste

For salad:

12 cups romaine lettuce

1 ½ cups chopped tomatoes

6 tablespoons shredded, cheddar cheese

6 tablespoons keto friendly thousand island dressing

Instructions

1. For burger crumble: Place a nonstick pan over medium heat. Add beef and garlic and sauté until brown. Break it simultaneously as it cooks. Drain excess fat from the pan.

2. Add Worcestershire sauce, pepper and seasoning salt and mix well.

3. Lower heat and simmer for 3-4 minutes. Stir frequently while cooking. Remove from heat.

4. To assemble: Place 4 cups lettuce leaves on each serving plate. Place ½ cup beef burger crumbles on it. Top with tomatoes and 2 tablespoons Thousand Island dressing. Sprinkle 2 tablespoons cheese on top.

5. Serve immediately.

CHAPTER ELEVEN

KETO LUNCH RECIPES

EASY WHITE TURKEY CHILI

Makes 4 servings

Ingredients

1 lb. ground turkey (pork, lamb or ground beef)

1 large head of cauliflower

2 tablespoons coconut oil

1 small white onion, finely chopped

2 garlic cloves, crushed

2 cups milk (full fat)

1 tablespoon mustard

1 teaspoon garlic powder, thyme, black pepper, celery salt

Instructions

1. Wash the cauliflower head thoroughly under some running water and pat it dry. Now rice it using a shredder. Keep aside.

2. Heat some coconut oil on medium flame in a large pot.

3. Now add the crushed garlic and chopped onion to the pot and sauté until slightly golden brown.

4. Add the ground turkey and stir it for about 2-3 minutes using a large spatula.

5. Slide in the cauliflower rice, seasoning and stir all the ingredients well.

6. Once the meat starts turning nice and brown, slowly add the coconut milk to the pot while stirring it continuously with a large wooden spoon.

7. Bring the mixture to a boil and then lower the flame to allow it to simmer for 8 minutes while stirring it occasionally.

8. Once the mixture is reduced by half and has turned thick, it's time to serve.

9. Pour the mixture into large soup bowls and add some generous amounts of shredded cheese on top.

10. Serve.

SPINACH AND FETA TURKEY BURGERS

Makes 4 servings

Ingredients

1 large egg

1 ounce feta cheese

20 ounces ground turkey

¼ teaspoon garlic paste

1/2 ounces frozen chopped spinach

Salt to taste

Pepper to taste

Instructions

1. Add all the ingredients into a bowl. Mix well.

2. Divide the mixture into 4 equal portions and shape into patties.

3. Cook on a preheated grill until it is not pink any more in the center of the burger. Cook on both the sides.

4. Serve with keto bun and toppings of your choice.

EGGPLANT AND BACON ALFREDO

Makes 3 servings

Ingredients

½ pound bacon, chopped

½ cup heavy whipping cream

1 large clove garlic

½ tablespoon lemon juice

¾ pound eggplant peeled, julienned

1 tablespoon butter

½ tablespoon white wine

½ cup parmesan cheese, shredded

A handful fresh basil, chopped

Instructions

1. Place a skillet over medium heat. Add bacon and cook until it becomes crisp. Remove the bacon with a slotted spoon and place on a plate that is lined with paper towels. Retain the fat in the pan.

2. Add eggplant to the pan and cook until it becomes tender. Make a depression in the center of the pan and add butter.

3. Toss well. Add garlic and toss again. Add heavy whipping cream, white wine and lemon juice and fold gently.

4. Add Parmesan cheese and half the bacon. Stir until well combined.

5. Turn off the heat. Sprinkle basil. Top with remaining bacon.

6. Serve.

BAKED CHICKEN

Makes 4 servings

Ingredients

2 medium chicken breasts, halved

1 ½ cups baby spinach, chopped

½ cup roasted red pepper

1 ½ tablespoon butter

6 tablespoons light cream cheese

1 ½ tablespoon low fat Parmesan cheese, shredded

Salt to taste

Pepper powder to taste

Any herbs and spices of your choice

Instructions

1. Pound the chicken breasts pieces with a meat mallet to make cutlets.
2. Add cream cheese, Parmesan, and red pepper into a bowl and mix well.
3. Heat butter in a nonstick skillet. Add spinach. Sauté for a few minutes until the spinach wilts. Remove and add the spinach to the cheese mixture.
4. Add salt, pepper, and herbs. Mix well.
5. Slather a large spoonful of the mixture over each of the chicken cutlets.
6. Roll the cutlets tightly and place with its seam side down on a greased pan.
7. Sprinkle salt and pepper over it.
8. Bake in a preheated oven at 400° F for about 45-60 minutes.
9. Remove from the oven. Serve after 10 minutes.

TUNA BOWL WITH AVOCADO AND NOODLE RICE

Makes 2 servings

Ingredients

½ pound fresh ahi tuna, cut into small cubes

1 small avocado, peeled, pitted, cubed

½ bag miracle noodle rice

½ tablespoon sesame oil

1 tablespoon soy sauce

½ jalapeños (optional), finely chopped

¼ cup edamame, shelled

½ bunch scallion, finely chopped

½ tablespoon black sesame seeds

½ tablespoon white sesame seeds

Instructions

1. Add soy sauce and sesame oil in a bowl and whisk well. Add tuna and toss well. Refrigerate for an hour.

2. Rinse the miracle noodle rice for 10-15 seconds.

3. Place a small saucepan with water over medium heat. Bring to the boil. Add miracle rice and boil for 2 minutes. Drain and transfer rice into a pan.

4. Place the pan over medium heat. Cook until dry.

5. Add avocado into a bowl. Add edamame, scallion, jalapeño, tuna and miracle noodle rice and toss well.

6. To make Saravo sauce: Add mayonnaise, lime juice and sriracha sauce into a bowl and mix well. Add sauce into the bowl of tuna and fold gently.

7. Divide into bowls. Sprinkle both the sesame seeds over it and serve.

Salt to taste

Pepper to taste

For Saravo sauce:

1 ½ tablespoons mayonnaise

1-2 teaspoons lime juice

½ teaspoon sriracha sauce

LOW CARB KETO LASAGNA

Makes 6 servings

Ingredients

1 tablespoon ghee

½ lb. Italian sausage

15 oz. ricotta cheese

2 tablespoons coconut flour

1 large whole egg

1 ½ teaspoon sea salt

½ teaspoon ground black pepper

1 teaspoon garlic powder

1 large garlic clove finely chopped

1 ½ cup mozzarella cheese

1/3 cup parmesan cheese

4 large zucchinis, thinly sliced

1 tablespoon mixed her seasoning

Instructions

1. Take the sliced zucchini and sprinkle some salt over it and toss well using two separate spoons. Place the salted zucchini to a big paper towel and allow it to sit for 30 minutes. Once the time is up, take the zucchini and place it on another paper towel, wrap it up and press it using both hands. You want to make sure that all the moisture is extracted from the zucchini as much as possible. Set aside.

2. Melt some butter in a large pan over low flame. IN the meanwhile, crumble the sausage using your hands and add it to the pan. Fry it for 5-6 minutes until nice and brown. Now remove from pan and allow it to cool off.

3. Preheat the oven to 375 degrees. Line a baking tray with some parchment paper.

4. In a bowl, add some ricotta cheese, 1 cup mozzarella, 2 tablespoons parmesan cheese, garlic powder, pepper, salt, coconut flour, egg and mix all the ingredients well using a large spoon.

5. Add a layer of sliced zucchini at the bottom of the baking dish. Now spread the cheese mixture on top and sprinkle some red pepper flakes and mixed herb seasoning on it. Repeat this process with the remaining zucchini 3-4 times until all the ingredients are exhausted.

1 teaspoon red pepper flakes

¼ cup fresh basil leaves, chopped

6. Finally, add the remaining cheeses on top, cover the dish with a foil, and bake in the oven for 30 minutes.

7. Remove the foil, check if done or else bake for another 15 minutes until golden brown.

8. Remove from oven and allow it to sit for 10 minutes before you serve.

9. Garnish with some chopped basil leaves and serve.

STEAK WITH MUSHROOM PORT SAUCE

Makes 4 servings

Ingredients

4 lbs Rib eye steak

4 ounces heavy cream

2 tablespoons butter

20 ounces mushrooms

8 ounces port wine

Salt to taste

Pepper to taste

Instructions

1. Season the steak with salt and pepper.

2. Place a large cast iron skillet over high heat. Add butter. When butter melts, place steak and cook for 2 minutes on each side.

3. Place the skillet into a preheated oven.

4. Bake at 450°F for 15-20 minutes or until the internal temperature of the meat shows 135°F when checked with a cooking thermometer. Flip sides half way through baking.

5. Remove the skillet from the oven. Remove the steak, cover with foil and set aside for a while.

6. Pour port wine into the skillet. Scrape the bottom of the skillet to remove any browned bits.

7. Place the skillet over medium heat. Add mushrooms and cream and bring to the boil. Simmer until mushrooms are tender.

8. Spoon the sauce over steak and serve.

BBQ PULLED BEEF SANDO

Makes 4 servings

Ingredients

3 lb. boneless chuck roast

2 teaspoons Himalayan pink salt

2 teaspoons garlic powder

1 teaspoon onion powder

1 teaspoon black pepper powder

1 tablespoon smoked paprika

2 tablespoons tomato paste

¼ cup apple cider vinegar

2 tablespoons coconut aminos

½ cup bone broth

¼ cup butter

Instructions

1. Clean the chuck roast properly using paper towels. Using a sharp kitchen knife, trim the excess fat off the roast and slice it up into two large pieces. Set aside on a large plate.

2. In a bowl, combine some paprika, garlic powder, onion powder, black pepper powder, smoked paprika, salt and mix well. Now rub some olive oil over the chuck roast and then coat it generously with the above mixture. Use your hands so you can coat both the roast pieces well with the herb mixture.

3. Place the beef pieces in a slow cooker.

4. Melt some butter on low heat in a small pan and allow it to cool off.

5. Add it to a bowl. To this, add vinegar, tomato paste, and coconut aminos and mix well.

6. Now pour this mixture all over the beef, which is placed in the cooker.

7. Close the lid of the cooker and cook it on low for about 10-12 hours. Once the time is up, open the lid, remove the beef and set the temperature to high. Allow the sauce to thicken.

8. Shred the beef using a sharp kitchen knife and then add it back to the cooker.

9. Toss it using two separate large spoons and toss well along with the sauce.

10. Serve immediately.

BROCCOLI WITH ITALIAN SAUSAGE

Makes 4 servings

Ingredients

16 ounces Italian sausage

4 cloves garlic, thinly sliced

4 tablespoons Parmesan cheese, grated

2 tablespoons olive oil

8 cups raw broccoli rabe, chopped

Salt to taste

Pepper to taste

Instructions

1. Place a pot of water with a teaspoon of salt over medium heat. Bring to the boil.
2. Add broccoli rabe and cook for a couple of minutes until it gets bright green in color.
3. Drain in a colander.
4. Place a large skillet over medium heat. Add sausage and cook until done.
5. Add oil and garlic and sauté until fragrant.
6. Stir in the drained broccoli rabe and sauté for 2-3 minutes. Turn off the heat.
7. Sprinkle salt and pepper. Sprinkle Parmesan cheese on top and serve right away.

ENCHILADA STYLE STUFFED PEPPERS

Makes 5 servings

Ingredients

2 lb. ground beef (85% lean pastured beef)

1 cup frozen cauliflower rice

3 tablespoons butter

1 small white onion, chopped

1 large carrot

2 garlic cloves, crushed

2 teaspoons smoked sea salt

2 teaspoons beberé

5 large bell peppers

5 dollops of sour cream, preferably organic

Instructions

1. Wash the carrots thoroughly under some running water and pat them dry using paper towels. Slice them up finely using a sharp kitchen knife. Set aside.

2. Clean the beef properly using paper towels. Using a sharp kitchen knife, trim the excess fat off the roast and set aside.

3. Heat a large pan on medium heat and melt some butter in it.

4. Slide in the garlic and onion and sauté until golden brown.

5. Throw in the carrots and sauté for about 7-8 minutes until tender.

6. Now add the beef along with some salt and break the beef until it is crumbed and then brown it.

7. Add the cauliflower rice, toss well and fry for a minute. Remove the pan from the heat.

8. Preheat the oven to 400 degrees F. While the oven is heating up, with the help of a knife, gently cut off the top of the bell peppers, and remove the seeds and core.

9. Now spoon the beef mixture inside each of these bell peppers and place them in a casserole dish.

10. Sprinkle a little berbere spice mix on top.

11. Bake in the oven for 40 minutes.

12. Garnish with generous amounts of sour cream on top and serve.

LEMON HERB LOW CARB KETO LOAF

Makes 6 servings

Ingredients

2 lb. ground beef (85% lean)

½ tablespoon pink salt

1 teaspoon ground black pepper

1/4 cup nutritional yeast

2 large eggs

2 tablespoons avocado oil

1 tablespoon lemon zest

¼ cup freshly chopped parsley

¼ cup freshly chopped oregano

4 garlic cloves

Instructions

1. Preheat the oven to 400 degrees Fahrenheit.

2. In a large bowl, add the ground beef along with some pepper, salt, and nutritional yeast and mix well. Set aside.

3. In a food processor or a blender, add the herbs, oil and garlic. Now give the mixture a whisk until the eggs are nice and frothy while the lemon, garlic and herbs are mixed and minced.

4. Gently crack the egg into the beef mixture and mix well using a spoon to combine.

5. Grease a large baking dish with some cooking oil or line it with a parchment paper. Add the beef to it evenly and flatten it out using a spoon.

6. Set the dish inside the oven and bake for about 50-60 minutes.

7. Once done, remove the dish from the oven and gently tilt the baking pan over the sink for draining out the excess fluid. Allow it to cool off for about 5-10 minutes before cutting it into slices.

8. Garnish with some lemon wedges and serve immediately.

LOW CARB KETO CHILI

Makes 6 servings

Ingredients

½ tablespoon avocado oil

2 ribs celery, finely chopped

2 lb. ground beef (85% lean)

1 tablespoon chipotle chili powder

2 tablespoons garlic powder

1 tablespoon chili powder

1 tablespoon cumin

1 teaspoon ground black pepper

1 teaspoon salt

1 large can thick tomato sauce

4 cups beef broth

Instructions

1. Heat some avocado oil in a large pot over medium heat. Slide in some chopped celery and cook for about 3-4 minutes until softened. Remove the celery in a bowl and set aside.

2. Add some ground beef in the same pan along with some chili powder, cumin, garlic powder, chipotle chili powder and mix well using a large wooden spoon. Now brown the beef until it is nice and brown.

3. Reduce the heat to low and empty a can of tomato sauce in the pot.

4. Slowly add the beef broth to the pot and stir again. Allow the mixture to simmer for about 10 minutes while stirring it occasionally.

5. Slide in the celery back to the pot and mix well.

6. Season with some salt and pepper and serve.

SUPER FOOD MEATBALLS

Makes 10 servings

Ingredients

3 lb. ground beef (85% lean)

1 lb. chicken livers (pastured)

1 large shallot

4 medium carrots

3 large garlic cloves

2 tablespoons grass fed butter

1 teaspoon dried oregano

2 tablespoons coconut aminos (separated)

3 teaspoons salt

2 teaspoons ground black pepper

1 tablespoon dried thyme

1 tablespoon garlic powder

1 tablespoon olive oil

Instructions

1. Heat some olive oil in a large pan on medium heat.
2. Until then, wash the carrots and pat them dry using paper towels. Now using a sharp knife mince them together with the shallots and garlic until fine.
3. Now slide in the garlic into the pan and sauté until golden.
4. Add carrots, shallots and cook for about 7-8 minutes until tender.
5. Now add the chicken livers followed by dried oregano and about 1 teaspoon of salt.
6. Allow the livers to cook until they are completely browned.
7. Add about 1-tablespoon coconut aminos and some apple cider vinegar and cook the mixture until half and the livers are tender.
8. Allow it to cool off and then transfer the mixture to a food processor and pulse until it resembles ground beef. Transfer to a large bowl to cool off.
9. Preheat the oven to 425 degrees F.
10. Add the beef mixture to a large bowl along with the rest of the seasoning and some salt. Using your hands combine the mixture and roll out 1 ½ inch shaped meatballs (approx. 30).

11. Add the meatballs to a greased baking pan and drizzle some olive oil on top. Then lightly drizzle them with the coconut aminos on top.

12. Place the pan in the oven and bake for 5 minutes at 425 degrees F. Later, turn down the temperature to 350 degrees F.

13. Roast for another 20 minutes and then remove it from the oven.

1 You can simply dunk these meatballs into some ranch or drizzle some lemon tahini sauce for added flavor and serve.

ROASTED CHICKEN STACKS

Makes 5 servings

Ingredients

5 small pieces of chicken breasts

1 small head cabbage

5 slices of prosciutto

3 tablespoons coconut flour

2 teaspoons salt

1 teaspoon ground black pepper

2 teaspoon Italian herb mix

½ cup bone broth

¼ cup avocado oil

Instructions

1. Preheat the oven to 400 degrees F.

2. Clean the chicken properly using paper towels and trim excess fat if any using a kitchen knife.

3. Now add the chicken to a gallon sized plastic bag along with some salt, pepper, coconut flour and herbs and shake the bag well to evenly coat the chicken.

4. Drizzle a bit of oil on the sheet pan.

5. Wash the cabbage thoroughly under running water and pat it dry. Now shred it using a sharp kitchen knife. Make about 5 piles of shredded cabbage on the pan. Sprinkle a bit of salt, and drizzle some oil on top.

6. Now gently place one coated chicken breast over each of them.

7. Finally, top the chicken with a slice of prosciutto. Drizzle the remaining oil on top.

8. Roast in the oven for 30 minutes at 400 degrees F.

9. Pour the chicken broth in the pan and roast for about 10 minutes.

10. Remove the chicken from the oven and serve immediately.

CURRY CHICKEN LETTUCE WRAPS

Makes 2 servings

Ingredients

1 lb. chicken thighs, boneless

¼ cup minced onion

2 garlic cloves, finely chopped

2 teaspoons curry powder

1 ½ teaspoon Himalayan salt

1 teaspoon black pepper

3 tablespoons butter or ghee

Half cauliflower head

6-8 small lettuce leaves

¼ cup unsweetened coconut milk yogurt

Instructions

1. Wash the cauliflower head thoroughly under some running water and pat it dry. Now rice it using a shredder. Keep aside.

2. Prepare all your veggies and set them aside.

3. Heat a pan on medium flame. Melt some ghee in it and then add the minced onion. Sauté until golden brown.

4. Slide in the chicken along with some salt and garlic and stir well.

5. Cook the chicken for about 8-9 minutes until nice and brown and tender.

6. Add in some more ghee if you wish along with the cauliflower rice and curry powder.

7. Wash the lettuce leaves properly and pat them dry. Now lay them on a large plate and fill in the curry chicken mixture into each one of them.

8. Top the wrap with a dollop of cream, secure it with a toothpick and serve.

LEMON BALSAMIC CHICKEN WITH ZOODLES

Makes 6 servings

Ingredients

8 large pieces of chicken thighs

3 tablespoons butter (pastured)

1 cup sliced onion

1 cup purple cabbage, shredded

2 tablespoons lemon rind

2 bay leaves

2 teaspoons pink Himalayan salt

1 teaspoon dried Italian herb blend

1 teaspoon ground black pepper

1 ½ tablespoon balsamic vinegar

5 tablespoons olive oil

Instructions

1. Heat your cooker on sauté mode and add in about 2 tablespoons of butter

2. Once the butter starts melting, slide in the sliced onion and sauté until golden brown.

3. Add the onion, lemon and cabbage into the cooker and sauté until it turns tender.

4. Clean the chicken thighs with paper towels and trim excess fat is any.

5. Slide in the chicken into the cooker along with bay leaves and seasoning. Stir the chicken well using a large wooden spoon. Allow the chicken t cook away for 3-4 minutes until tender.

6. Add in the vinegar and stir again. Cancel the sauté function and then close the lid. Set it to poultry and cook for 20 minutes on high.

7. Once the chicken is cooked properly, allow the pressure to release naturally. Open the lid and allow all the steam to pass. Remove the chicken from the cooker and onto a plate. Now, using two separate forks shred the chicken properly.

8. Mix in the remaining tablespoon of butter and add this yummy and saucy chicken over the zoodles.

9. Drizzle some avocado or olive oil on top and serve.

MEXICAN SHREDDED BEEF

Makes 6 servings

Ingredients

2 – 2 ½ lbs chuck roast

2 tablespoons bacon fat or lard

½ cup water

2 cloves garlic, minced

½ teaspoon chipotle chili powder or ½ tablespoon chili powder

Salt to taste

Pepper to taste

7 1/2 ounces canned diced tomatoes

1 tablespoon liquid smoke (optional)

½ teaspoon ground cumin

Instructions

1. Place the rack in the oven in the position next to the lowest position.

2. Sprinkle salt and pepper generously over the roast.

3. Place a Dutch oven over medium heat. Add bacon fat. When it melts, place the roast and cook until brown on all the sides.

4. Add rest of the ingredients and stir. Bring to the boil.

5. Lower heat and simmer until the roast is tender. It will take 3-4 hours. You can also place it in a crockpot and cook.

6. When done, remove the roast and place on your cutting board. When cool enough to handle, shred with a pair of forks. Add the meat into the pot and heat thoroughly.

7. Serve hot over cauliflower rice.

CREAMY MUSHROOM CHICKEN

Makes 2 servings

Ingredients

2 large chicken cutlets

1 tablespoon olive oil

1 small white onion

5 cremini mushrooms

½ teaspoon pink salt

½ teaspoon dried thyme

3 tablespoons butter

1/3 cup full fat coconut milk

Instructions

1. Clean the chicken properly using paper towels and trim excess fat if any. Season it with some salt and pepper and allow it to marinate. Set aside.

2. Heat a large pan with about two tablespoons of butter in it and allow it to melt.

3. Once done, slide in the mushrooms, sprinkle a bit of salt and sauté until the mushrooms are tender. Keep stirring often so the mushrooms don't turn completely brown.

4. Throw in the sliced onions and keep stirring the mixture using a big wooden spoon for about 5-6 minutes. Now remove the onion and mushroom mixture from the pan on to a dish.

5. Add a little of butter to the pan again, and allow it to melt.

6. Place all the chicken cutlets on the pan one by one and cook them for about 5 minutes on each side until they are brown and crispy.

7. Now add the onion and mushroom mixture back to the pan and slowly pour the coconut milk on top of it. Ensure that you shake the coconut milk can thoroughly so there is a god mix of fat when you are adding it to the pan.

8. Allow it to simmer for a minute, remove and serve immediately.

MUSHROOM BACON SKILLET

Makes 2 servings

Ingredients

4 large slices of bacon

2 cup mixed mushrooms, halved (a mix of cremini, shitake and ali'i)

½ teaspoon pink salt

1 tablespoon garlic powder

Instructions

1. Heat a large pan over medium heat. If you wish you can drizzle a bit of olive oil to grease the pan.

2. Now start preparing your ingredients

3. Cut the bacon slice into 1-inch pieces.

4. Take the stems off the thyme leaves.

5. Add the bacon slices to the pan and cook for about 3-4 minutes until they are nice and crispy while stirring them continuously. Make sure you don't burn them. Now add the mushrooms and sauté them until slightly brown.

6. Sprinkle some salt, garlic powder, thyme and keep stirring and cooking until all the flavors start releasing.

7. Once all the ingredients get blended in, remove from heat and transfer on to a large plate.

8. Serve along with some boiled eggs or onion greens on the side.

SHRIMP STIR FRY WITH BAKED CAULIFLOWER RICE

Makes 4 servings

Ingredients

1 lb. shrimp, tail on

2 inch ginger root

4 stalks of green onion

2 large garlic cloves

4 baby bella mushrooms

½ teaspoon lemon rind

2 teaspoons Himalayan pink salt

3 tablespoons bacon fat

2 tablespoons MCT oil

Half a head of small cauliflower

Instructions

1. Wash the cauliflower head thoroughly under some running water and pat it dry. Now rice it using a shredder. Keep aside.

2. Preheat the oven to 400 degrees F.

3. Spread the cauliflower rice on a baking tray, drizzle some MCT oil over it and sprinkle some pink salt on top.

4. Place the dish inside the oven and bake for 10 minutes until nice and slightly brown.

5. Slice the ginger root and garlic clove using a kitchen knife. Similarly, finely slice up the green onion.

6. Heat a pan on low flame. Now add in the bacon fat, garlic, ginger, lemon rind, green onion and sauté for about 2-3 minutes on low flame.

7. Slide in the shrimps and sauté them for 3-4 minutes while stirring them continuously so they don't turn chewy.

8. Add the coconut aminos along with some salt and stir for another 2-3 minutes.

9. Spread the baked cauliflower rice on a large plate. Add the shrimp mixture on top and garnish with

some sesame seeds, green onion and chili flakes and serve.

LOW CARB CRISPY FRIED CHICKEN

Makes 4 servings

Ingredients

2 tablespoons avocado oil

1 cup sunflower seeds

½ cup sesame seeds

1 teaspoon pink salt

1 teaspoon ground black pepper

1 teaspoon dried Italian herbs

1 lb. boneless chicken thighs, 8 pieces

Instructions

1. Preheat the oven to 425 degrees F.
2. Grease a baking pan with some oil.
3. In a blender or a food processor, grind the sesame seeds, sunflower seeds and seasonings and turn them into a crumbly mixture. Remember not to over blend them, as we need a texture that resembles breadcrumbs. You can also use the whisk and stop method. Whisk it for 2 seconds and then stop, and repeat this process until you get a crumbly texture.
4. Add this mixture to a container or a freezer bag.
5. Now pick the chicken thighs one by one and add them to freezer bag and shake the bag to coat them well with the seed mixture. Repeat this with all the chicken thighs.
6. Place the chicken thigh on a baking tray and drizzle some avocado oil on it.
7. Roast them for 30 minutes while turning the chicken thighs over after every few minutes using tongs.
8. Season them with some salt and ground pepper and serve.

THE PERFECT KETO LUNCH

Makes 4 servings

Ingredients

4 large eggs

24 asparagus spears

12 large slices of bacon, pastured

Instructions

1. Preheat the oven to 400 degrees F.

2. Using a knife, trim the bottom of the asparagus, like about half inch from down and wrap each of the sticks with a slice of bacon. Make sure that you hold the spears firmly with one hand while you start winding each slice of the bacon right from the bottom of the spear to the top. Gently pull the bacon slice as you are wrapping them around the asparagus sticks. Place them on a pan.

3. Place the pan in the oven and bake for 20 minutes until they are nice and crispy.

4. In the meanwhile, fill a small pot with water and bring it to a boil. Insert 4 eggs in the water and allow them to boil for about 6 minutes.

5. In a bowl full of icy cold water, add the eggs and allow them to sit for about 2 minutes so you can peel them easily.

6. Gently crack the egg by tapping it on a hard surface and then using your hands, peel the shell off the eggs.

7. With the help of a small spoon, scoop out the top of the eggs to unveil a perfectly runny yolk.

8. Now simply dip the asparagus sticks into the eggs and enjoy.

TURKEY SAUSAGE FRITTATA

Makes 8 servings

Ingredients

12 oz. ground breakfast sausage, preferably turkey

2 large bell peppers

12 large eggs

1 cup sour cream, lactose free

1 teaspoon Himalayan pink salt

1 teaspoon ground black pepper

2 teaspoons butter

2 oz. shredded cheddar

Instructions

1. Preheat the oven to 350 degrees F.

2. Carefully crack all your eggs in a blender one by one. Add a bit of salt, some pepper and sour cream and blend it for 30 seconds on high until it forms a nice and frothy mixture. Set aside.

3. Heat a large pan on medium flame. Add some butter and allow it to melt.

4. Using a knife, slice the bell peppers and add them to the pan. Sauté for about 3-4 minutes until they are tender. Remove them from the pan.

5. Slide in the turkey sausage, stir and cook for about 8 minutes until brown. Flatten the turkey and place them at the bottom of the baking dish. Add cooked peppers on top. Now slowly pour the egg mix on top.

6. Place the baking dish inside the oven and bake for 30 minutes.

7. As soon as the Frittata is done, remove it from the oven and quickly sprinkle the cheddar cheese on top so it melts away.

8. Serve.

CHAPTER TWELVE

KETO DINNER – RECIPES

CREAMY TUSCAN GARLIC CHICKEN

Makes 2-3 servings

Ingredients

¾ lb chicken breasts, skinless, boneless, thinly sliced

½ cup heavy cream

½ teaspoon garlic powder

¼ cup parmesan cheese

¼ cup sun-dried tomatoes

1 tablespoon olive oil

¼ cup chicken broth

½ teaspoon Italian seasoning

½ cup chopped spinach

Instructions

1. Place a skillet over medium heat. Add oil and heat. Add chicken and cook until the underside is golden brown. Flip sides and cook until brown.

2. Remove chicken with a slotted spoon and set aside in a bowl.

3. Add broth, cream garlic powder, Parmesan cheese and Italian seasoning into the same skillet. Raise the heat to medium- high heat. Stir constantly until well combined and thick.

4. Stir in the spinach and sundried tomatoes. Simmer for a few minutes until spinach wilts.

5. Place the chicken back in the skillet. Mix well.

6. Serve over keto friendly pasta if desired, like zucchini noodles, kelp noodles etc.

GRILLED CHICKEN AND SPINACH PIZZA

Makes 4 servings

Ingredients

2 chicken breasts, skinless, boneless

2 cloves garlic, minced

½ teaspoon xanthan gum

1 cup part skim mozzarella cheese, shredded

1 tablespoon olive oil

1 cup half and half or heavy whipping cream

2 cups fresh spinach, chopped

Pepper to taste

Sea salt to taste

For pizza crust:

40 ounces cream cheese

2 eggs, beaten

2/3 cup almond flour

Instructions

1. To make pizza crust: Add cream cheese and mozzarella cheese into a microwave safe bowl.

2. Microwave on high for 1-2 minutes. Stir every 30 seconds until completely melted.

3. Meanwhile, add egg, almond flour and garlic powder into a bowl. Whisk well.

4. Add melted cheese mixture into it. Mix until dough is formed.

5. Cover and refrigerate for a while.

6. Place a skillet over medium heat. Add oil and heat, add chicken and cook until tender.

7. Remove chicken with a slotted spoon and set aside on a plate. When cool enough to handle, shred or chop the chicken.

8. Add garlic, xanthan gum and half and half into the skillet.

9. When it begins to boil, lower the heat and simmer until thick. Stir frequently.

10. Add spinach and stir. Cook until spinach wilts. Turn off the heat.

11. Place dough into a greased pizza pan. Press it well onto the bottom of the pan.

1 ½ cups mozzarella cheese, shredded

½ teaspoon garlic powder

12. Bake in a preheated oven at 350° F for about 10-15 minutes.

13. Spread the spinach mixture over the crust.

14. Scatter chicken over the crust. Sprinkle cheese on top.

15. Bake for 5-6 minutes until the cheese melts.

16. Cut into wedges and serve.

ZUCCHINI PASTA WITH CHICKEN & PISTACHIOS

Makes 2-3 servings

Ingredients

For noodles:

1 lb zucchini

½ tablespoon extra-virgin olive oil

A large pinch ground cumin

½ tablespoon salt

1 clove garlic, peeled, crushed

Pepper to taste

For chicken:

2 chicken breasts, skinless, boneless

½ teaspoon salt

½ tablespoon extra-virgin olive oil or ghee

Instructions

1. Make noodles of the zucchini using a spiralizer or a julienne peeler.

2. Place a colander over a bowl and the zucchini in the colander. Sprinkle salt and toss well. Let the moisture from the noodles drain for 20-30 minutes.

3. To make chicken: Place chicken between 2 pieces of plastic wrap. Pound with a meat mallet until ½ inch thick. Cut into strips, crosswise.

4. Place a skillet over medium-high heat. Add oil and heat. Season chicken with salt and pepper and place in the skillet, in a single layer.

5. Cook for 2-3 minutes without stirring. Flip sides and cook the other side for 2-3 minutes. Repeat with the other sides. Turn off the heat.

6. Remove chicken with a slotted spoon and place on a plate. Cover with foil, loosely.

7. Add all the aromatics into a bowl. Sir with a fork and set aside.

8. Finishing: Add oil, garlic, cumin and pepper into a bowl. Sir with a fork and set aside.

¼ teaspoon pepper

For aromatics:

1 scallion, sliced

2 tablespoons shelled pistachio nuts

5-6 mint leaves, minced

½ tablespoon lemon juice

9. Place the zucchini noodles under cold running water and rinse them well. Drain and place on a kitchen towel. Squeeze to remove excess moisture.

10. Place the skillet back over heat. Add noodles and cook until slightly tender. Move the noodles to one side of the skillet.

11. Lower the heat to medium low. Pour the garlic oil and let it heat for about half a minute. Stir constantly.

12. Move the noodles back to the center and toss well so that the oil is well coated on the noodles.

13. Remove from heat. Add chicken and pistachio mixture and toss well.

14. Divide into bowls and serve.

CHICKEN CLUB STUFFED AVOCADOES

Makes 2 servings

Ingredients

3 ounces grilled, chicken, diced

1 avocado, halved, pitted

2 slices cooked bacon, crumbled, divided

2 tablespoons lime juice

2 tablespoons keto friendly mayonnaise

Salt to taste

Pepper to taste

1 small tomato, diced

A handful cilantro, chopped

Instructions

1. Carefully scoop the avocado flesh from the avocado halves but retain the avocado cases.

2. Add the scooped avocado into a bowl and mash it with a fork.

3. Add chicken, most of the bacon, 1-tablespoon lime juice, tomato, mayonnaise, half the cilantro, salt and pepper and mix well.

4. Fill this mixture in the avocado cases. Sprinkle remaining bacon and cilantro on top. Drizzle remaining lime juice on top and serve.

KALE AND TURKEY SAUSAGE SAUTÉ

Makes 4 servings

Ingredients

2 bunches kale, discard hard stems and ribs, cut into bite size pieces

4 cloves garlic, minced

½ cup shredded parmesan cheese

4 teaspoons olive oil

1 lb turkey sausage, discard casings

¼ teaspoon red pepper flakes

2 tablespoons lemon juice or to taste

Instructions

1. Place sausage in a large skillet and place skillet over medium-high heat.

2. Sprinkle salt and pepper and cook until brown. Break it simultaneously as it cooks.

3. Remove with a slotted spoon and place on a plate.

4. Add oil and heat. Add garlic and sauté until aromatic. Add red pepper flakes and stir for 5-6 seconds.

5. Add kale and sauté until kale wilts. Sprinkle salt and pepper and stir.

6. Stir in the browned sausage and mix well.

7. Sprinkle Parmesan cheese and lemon juice and mix well.

8. Serve hot.

ZUCCHINI PIZZA BOATS

Makes 8 servings

Ingredients

8 zucchinis, halved lengthwise, scoop the flesh and seeds from the center

8 ounces button mushrooms, sliced

1 green bell pepper, chopped

A handful fresh basil, chopped (optional)

2 small cans keto friendly pizza sauce

1 large onion, chopped

4 cups shredded mozzarella cheese

2 teaspoons red chili flakes

For filling:

1 lb ground turkey

2 teaspoons garlic powder

Instructions

1. To make filling: Place a large skillet over medium-high heat. Add turkey, salt and all the spices and mix well. Break it simultaneously as it cooks. Cook until brown and cooked through. Turn off the heat.

2. Place zucchini on a lined baking sheet. Spoon some sauce inside each. Spread it evenly. Divide the filling equally and spread in the cavities of the zucchini boats.

3. Scatter mushrooms, green pepper, and red onions all over the turkey.

4. Sprinkle cheese on top.

5. Bake in a preheated oven at 400° F for about 10-15 minutes.

6. Garnish with basil and red chili flakes and serve.

2 teaspoons Italian seasoning

4 teaspoons olive oil

4 teaspoons fennel seeds

1 teaspoon salt or to taste

LEFTOVER TURKEY CASSEROLE

Makes 4 servings

Ingredients

11 ounces leftover, cooked, shredded, turkey breast (2 cups approximately)

¾ cup green beans

¼ small onion, chopped

2 tablespoons butter

1 tablespoon chopped parsley

4 brown mushrooms

½ small carrot, chopped

½ cup broccoli florets

½ cup shredded cheddar cheese

1 tablespoon crushed pork rinds

3 cloves garlic, sliced

For keto white sauce:

1 tablespoon butter

Instructions

1. Place a large skillet over medium heat. Add butter and melt. Stir in garlic, onion and carrots and cover with a lid. Let it cook for 2 to 3 minutes.

2. Stir in broccoli and mushrooms and cook for 2 minutes, covered.

3. Add turkey and mix well. Remove from heat. Transfer into a casserole dish.

4. To make white sauce: Place a small pan over medium heat. Add butter and melt. Add cream cheese and stir. As the cream cheese starts melting, add cream and stir until well incorporated.

5. Add nutmeg, salt and pepper. Pour into the casserole dish and stir.

6. Scatter cheddar cheese, parsley and pork rinds on top.

7. Bake in a preheated oven at 400° F for about 10-15 minutes or until golden brown on top.

6 ounces heavy cream

½ teaspoon salt

1/8 teaspoon ground nutmeg

3 1/2 ounces cream cheese, cubed

¼ cup grated parmesan cheese

¼ teaspoon pepper

JALAPEÑO CHEDDAR BURGERS

Makes 8 (7 ounces each burger) servings

Ingredients

3 ½ lbs turkey or beef

Salt to taste

Pepper to taste

4 ounces cheddar cheese, shredded

2 fresh jalapeños, deseeded if desired, chopped

¼ cup finely minced onion

½ cup cream cheese

½ teaspoon garlic powder

2 tablespoons olive oil

Keto friendly toppings of your choice

Instructions

1. Add cream cheese, garlic powder, cheddar cheese and jalapeño into a bowl and stir. Divide into 8 equal portions.

2. Add the meat, onion, salt and pepper into a bowl and mix well.

3. Divide the mixture into 8 equal portions.

4. Flatten one portion of the meat mixture on your palm. Place one portion of cream cheese mixture on the meat mixture. Enclose the cream cheese mixture in the meat mixture by bringing together the edges and shape into a patty.

5. Repeat the previous step and make the remaining burgers.

6. Grill the burgers on a preheated grill for 6-7 minutes per side or until the way you like it cooked.

BEEF SATAY AND PEANUT SAUCE

Makes 8 servings

Ingredients

For beef satay and marinade:

2 lbs flank steak or skirt steak, sliced into 1 ½ inch strips across the grain, horizontally

4 tablespoons tamari or coconut aminos

1 teaspoon ground coriander

4 tablespoons fish sauce

4 tablespoons Sukrin gold, powdered or swerve confectioners' or any other keto friendly sweetener of your choice to taste

For Thai peanut sauce:

½ cup smooth peanut butter or almond butter

4 teaspoons Thai chili garlic sauce or to taste

Instructions

1. Make beef satay as follows: Insert the skewers into the beef strips.

2. Add fish sauce, soy sauce and sukrin into a baking dish and mix well. Brush this mixture over the beef strips.

3. Sprinkle coriander over the meat and rub it well into it. Place it in the baking dish. Set aside for 20-30 minutes. Turn the skewers a couple of times while it is marinating.

4. To make Thai peanut sauce: Add peanut butter into a microwave safe bowl. Microwave on high until it melts. It may take 30-60 seconds. Stir after every 20 seconds.

5. Remove the bowl from the microwave and add Thai chili garlic sauce, Thai curry paste and sweetener and whisk well.

6. Shake the can of coconut milk and pour into the bowl. Whisk well. Cover and set aside for a while for the flavors to set in.

7. For grilling: Drizzle 2 tablespoons oil all over the beef. It should be well coated.

8. Take some aluminum foil and place below the skewers while grilling.

1 teaspoon Thai red curry paste or to taste

2/3 cup, canned full fat coconut milk

2 tablespoons Sukrin gold, powdered or swerve confectioners' or any other keto friendly sweetener of your choice to taste

Other ingredients:

2 tablespoons olive oil

Bamboo skewers soaked in water for a few hours

9. Remove the skewers from the marinade. Grill on a preheated grill on both the sides according to the way you like it cooked.

10. Serve beef satay with Thai coconut soup.

GARLIC BUTTER BRAZILIAN STEAK

Makes 2 servings

Ingredients

3 medium cloves garlic, peeled, smashed

¾ lb skirt steak, trimmed, cut into 2 pieces

1 tablespoon canola oil or vegetable oil

2 teaspoons chopped, fresh flat-leaf parsley

Kosher salt to taste

Freshly ground pepper to taste

2 tablespoons unsalted butter

Instructions

1. Place crushed garlic on your cutting board. Sprinkle a little salt on it and then mince.

2. Dry the steak by patting with paper towels. Sprinkle salt and pepper over it, liberally.

3. Place a heavy skillet over medium-high heat. Add oil. When the oil is well heated, place steak in the skillet and cook until the underside is brown. Flip sides and cook the other side until brown.

4. Remove with a slotted spoon and set aside on a plate. Slice if desired.

5. To make garlic butter: Place a small pan over low heat. Add butter and melt. Stir in the garlic and cook until light golden brown.

6. Drizzle garlic butter over the steak. Scatter parsley on top and serve.

BEEF AND MUSHROOM STUFFED PEPPERS

Makes 12 servings

Ingredients

32 ounces ground beef

1 medium onion, chopped

4 medium tomatoes, finely chopped

Juice of ½ lime

4 cups shredded mozzarella cheese

Pepper to taste

6 medium bell peppers, halved lengthwise, deseeded

4 cups sliced fresh mushrooms

2 tablespoons olive oil

2 teaspoons garlic, crushed

2 teaspoons dried oregano

Salt to taste

Instructions

1. Place a nonstick pan over medium heat. Add oil. When the oil heats, add onions and sauté until translucent. Add salt, pepper, garlic and beef and sauté for about 10 -12 minutes. Stir frequently.

2. Pour half the fat (that is in the pan) into a baking dish. Use this fat to grease the baking dish.

3. Add mushrooms, oregano, tomatoes and lemon juice into the pan and cook until the mushrooms are tender.

4. Fill the beef mixture into the peppers and place the peppers with the filled side facing up, in the baking dish. Sprinkle cheese on top.

5. Bake in a preheated oven 350° F for 30 minutes

EASY STEAK FAJITA

Makes 8 servings

Ingredients

For marinade:

½ cup oil

2 tablespoons chili powder

2 teaspoons paprika

½ cup fresh lime juice

2 teaspoons ground cumin

2 teaspoons minced garlic

Red pepper flakes to taste

For steak:

2 lbs beef flank steak, cut into strips

2 medium yellow onions, sliced

2 medium green bell peppers, sliced

2 medium red bell pepper, sliced

Instructions

1. Add all the ingredients for marinade into a large bowl and stir until well combined.

2. Sprinkle salt and pepper over steak and place in the marinade. Turn the steak around until well coated.

3. Cover and refrigerate for 2-4 hours.

4. Remove from the refrigerator 30 minutes before grilling.

5. Grease the grill grates and preheat the grill.

6. Remove steak from the marinade and place over the grill. Cook until the desired doneness. Remove from the grill and set aside.

7. Place a large skillet over medium heat. Add oil. When the oil melts, add all the bell peppers and onions along with salt and pepper and cook until crisp as well as tender.

8. Spoon into lettuce cups. Place grilled steak over the vegetables. Drizzle sour cream on top and serve.

2 medium green bell peppers, sliced

Salt to taste

Pepper to taste

4 tablespoons coconut oil

To serve:

Lettuce cups

Sour cream

PARMESAN CRUSTED PORK CHOPS

Makes 8 servings

Ingredients

8 pork chops, boneless, thawed

4 tablespoons avocado oil or olive oil

Salt to taste

Pepper to taste

For Parmesan crust:

1 cup grated parmesan cheese

2 tablespoons minced fresh parsley

1 teaspoon lemon zest

2 large eggs

1 cup crushed pork rinds

1 teaspoon minced garlic

4 teaspoons water

Instructions

1. Remove the pork chops from the refrigerator at least 30 minutes before preparing.

2. Dry the pork chops by patting with paper towels. Sprinkle salt and pepper over the pork chops.

3. Add eggs and water into a bowl and whisk well.

4. Add Parmesan cheese, pork rinds, garlic, lemon zest and parsley into a wide shallow bowl. Mix well with your hands until well combined.

5. Place a frying pan over medium heat. Add 2 tablespoons oil and let it heat.

6. Lift the pork chop with a fork and dip it in the beaten eggs. Coat it well. Shake to drop off excess egg.

7. Next dredge in the Parmesan cheese mixture. Place in the pan. Cook 2-3 at a time.

8. Cook each pork chop for 2 minutes on each side. (Use a timer set up for 2 minutes)

9. Repeat the steps 5-8 with the remaining pork chops.

10. Serve hot.

SAUSAGE, PEPPER AND CAULIFLOWER FRIED RICE

Makes 4-6 servings

Ingredients

1 head cauliflower, chopped into florets

1 yellow bell pepper, sliced

1 red bell pepper, sliced

1 green bell pepper, sliced

18 ounces smoked sausage, sliced

1 onion, sliced

6 tablespoons olive oil

1 teaspoon garlic powder or minced garlic

1 cup chicken broth

A handful fresh parsley, chopped

½ teaspoon red pepper flakes (optional)

Instructions

1. Add cauliflower into the food processor bowl. Process until rice like in texture.

2. Transfer into a microwave safe bowl. Microwave on High for 6-7 minutes until cauliflower is tender.

3. Place a large skillet over medium-high heat. Add 2 tablespoons oil. When the oil is heated, add sausage and sauté until brown all over. Remove with a slotted spoon and set aside.

4. Add remaining oil into the skillet. Add onions and peppers and cook until slightly tender.

5. Add garlic, salt, Italian seasoning and pepper and sauté for about a minute, until aromatic.

6. Add broth and stir. Cook for a minute.

7. Stir in paprika and cayenne pepper.

8. Add cauliflower rice and sausage and mix well. Add salt and pepper to taste. Heat thoroughly.

9. Sprinkle parsley on top and serve.

2 teaspoons Italian seasoning

Salt to taste

Freshly cracked pepper to taste

BBQ PORK THAI STYLE

Makes 4 servings

Ingredients

For the salad:

20 ounces pork, cooked, pulled

½ cup fresh cilantro, chopped

4 cups romaine lettuce

1 medium red bell pepper, chopped

For the Thai BBQ sauce:

4 tablespoons tomato paste

2 teaspoons creamy peanut butter

Zest of 1 lime

Juice of 1 lime

2 teaspoons red curry paste

½ teaspoon red pepper flakes

20 drops liquid Stevia

Instructions

1. To make sauce: Whisk together all the ingredients of the sauce in a bowl and set aside for a while for the flavors to set in.

2. Mix together in a bowl, lettuce, cilantro and red bell pepper.

3. Divide among 4 plates. Divide and place the pork over it. Pour sauce over the pork and serve.

5-6 tablespoons soy sauce or coconut aminos

¼ cup fresh cilantro, chopped

2 teaspoons five spice powder

3 tablespoons rice wine vinegar

2 teaspoons fish sauce

1 teaspoon mango extract

PORK EGG ROLL IN A BOWL

Makes 2 servings

Ingredients

1 tablespoon sesame oil

¼ cup chopped onion

½ lb ground pork

Salt to taste

Pepper to taste

2 cloves garlic, minced

3 green onions, sliced at an angle, keep the green and white part separate

¼ teaspoon ground ginger

½ tablespoon Sriracha sauce or chili garlic sauce, or to taste

1 ½ tablespoons coconut aminos

1 tablespoon sesame seeds, toasted

Instructions

1. Place a skillet over medium-high heat. Add oil and heat. Add onion, garlic and whites of the green onions and sauté until soft.

2. Stir in the pork, salt, pepper, ginger. Cook for a couple of minutes.

3. Add Sriracha sauce and cook until pork is thoroughly cooked.

4. Stir in the coleslaw mix, vinegar and coconut aminos and cook until coleslaw is slightly soft.

5. Divide into bowls. Sprinkle sesame seeds and green onions on top and serve.

7 ounces coleslaw (from a 14 ounce bag)

½ tablespoon rice wine vinegar

EASY PORK STIR FRY

Makes 8 servings

Ingredients

1 ½ lbs pork loin, cut into thin strips

2 tablespoons minced fresh ginger

24 ounces broccoli florets

2 bunches green onions or scallions, cut into 2 inch pieces

2 red bell peppers, cut into strips

2 tablespoons extra dry sherry

2 teaspoons arrowroot

3 tablespoons avocado or olive oil, divided

2 teaspoons sesame oil

2 teaspoons minced garlic

3 tablespoons swerve sweetener

Instructions

1. Add oil, pork, garlic and ginger in a bowl. Toss well.
2. Add sweetener, arrowroot, tamari, sesame oil and sherry into another bowl. Whisk well and set aside.
3. Place a wok over high heat. Add avocado oil and heat, swirl the wok so that the oil spreads.
4. Add pork and cook for a while, without stirring. When the bottom part turns white, stir the pork and cook until the pork is cooked through.
5. Transfer into a serving bowl.
6. Add broccoli into the wok. Place the other vegetables over the broccoli. Do not stir.
7. Cover and cook for a few minutes. Add pork and stir. Heat thoroughly.
8. If there is excess liquid in the wok, then remove the pork and vegetables with a slotted spoon and place in a serving bowl.
9. Boil the liquid until it thickens. Pour the thickened sauce over the stir-fry and serve.

4 tablespoons tamari or coconut aminos or tamari

Sesame seeds to sprinkle

Red pepper flakes to taste

BROILED LAMB AND BUTTER FENNEL

Makes 4 servings

Ingredients

For lamb:

1 large onion, sliced into ¼ inch thick rounds

1 lb lamb stew meat, cut into 1 inch cubes

For fennel:

¾ lb fennel bulb, cut into ¼ inch thick slices

1 cup water

12 tablespoons butter

Freshly ground pepper to taste

Sea salt to taste

Instructions

1. Add lamb and onion into the broiler pan.
2. Broil in a preheated oven on high for 5-6 minutes or until brown on top and pink from inside.
3. Season with salt and pepper and set aside.
4. Place a skillet over medium heat. Add butter and melt. Add fennel and cook for 4-5 minutes.
5. Add salt and water and stir. Cover tightly with a lid.
6. Cook until soft. Do not overcook.
7. Serve lamb with butter fennel.

LAMB CHOPS WITH HERB BUTTER

Makes 2 servings

Ingredients

4 lamb chops, at room temperature

½ tablespoon olive oil

½ tablespoon butter

Salt to taste

Pepper to taste

Lemon wedges to serve

For herb butter:

2.5 ounces butter, at room temperature

½ teaspoon garlic powder

½ teaspoon lemon juice

1 clove garlic, pressed

2 tablespoons finely chopped parsley

¼ teaspoon salt or to tast

Instructions

1. To make herb butter: Add all the ingredients for herb butter into a bowl. Stir and set aside for a while for the flavors to set in.

2. Sprinkle salt and pepper over the lamb chops.

3. Meanwhile, make lamb chops as follows: Place a pan over medium heat. Add oil and butter. When butter melts, place lamb chops in the pan and cook for 3-4 minutes on each side.

4. Place 2 lamb chops in each plate. Serve with lemon wedges and half the herb butter in each plate.

LAMB SOUVLAKI (GREEK LAMB SKEWERS)

Makes 6 servings

Ingredients

2 3/4 lbs lamb, fatty ones, chopped into medium size pieces

3 tablespoons chopped fresh rosemary, or 3 teaspoons dried rosemary

¼ cup lemon juice

1 teaspoon salt or to taste

¼ cup fresh mint, chopped or 2 teaspoons dried mint

¾ cup extra virgin olive oil

Instructions

1. Add olive oil, lemon juice, salt, mint, and rosemary into a bowl and mix well.

2. Add the lamb pieces and mix well. Marinate in the refrigerator for 5-8 hours. Stir a couple of times while it is marinating.

3. Thread the meat on to skewers. Place the skewers on the rack in a preheated oven.

4. Roast in a preheated oven 450° F for 15-20 minutes. Turn the skewers half way through roasting.

5. Remove from the oven. Let it cool for a couple of minutes.

6. Serve with Melitzanosalata or a keto friendly salad.

TURKISH LAMB & EGGPLANT KEBABS

Makes 2-3 servings

Ingredients

For Baharat (Turkish spice paste) and lamb:

1 tablespoon extra-virgin olive oil

½ tablespoon paprika

1 teaspoon garlic, minced

½ teaspoon salt or to taste

¼ teaspoon ground allspice

½ teaspoon ground cumin

A large pinch teaspoon ground cinnamon

1 tablespoon lemon juice

1 teaspoon tomato paste

½ teaspoon dried oregano

¼ teaspoon freshly ground pepper

Instructions

1. Add 1-tablespoon oil, garlic, paprika, lemon juice, oregano, tomato paste, salt, pepper, coriander, cumin, cinnamon, cayenne and allspice powder in a mixing bowl. Mix until well combined.

2. Set aside 1 tablespoon of this mixture in a separate bowl.

3. Coat the lamb with the remaining mixture.

4. Place lamb in a bowl. Mix well and refrigerate for 3-5 hours.

5. Preheat a grill to medium heat. You can use a charcoal grill too.

6. Meanwhile, make the kebabs as follows: Place the slices of eggplant on a baking sheet and sprinkle lightly with salt. Let it stand for 15 minutes.

7. Thread the onions and lamb on to skewers, alternately.

8. Rinse the eggplant and pat dry with paper towel.

9. Fix the eggplant horizontally on to skewers such that the eggplant lays flat on the grill, when the skewers are placed on the gill.

10. Mix the remaining 2 tablespoons oil to the spice paste mixture that was retained. Brush the eggplants with this mixture.

½ teaspoon ground coriander

¼ teaspoon cayenne pepper

1 lb boneless leg of lamb, trimmed and cut into 1 1/2-inch cubes

For kebabs:

2 Japanese or other small eggplant (about ½ lb), cut into 1/2-inch rounds

¼ teaspoon salt

1 medium red onion, cut into 1-inch chunks

2 tablespoon extra-virgin olive oil

Lemon wedges for serving

11. To grill: Place the skewers with the lamb in the center of the grill that is the hottest part of the grill and place the eggplants around the kebabs where the grill is comparatively cooler.

12. Turn the skewers a couple of times and cook until the lamb is golden brown outside and yet pink inside.

13. Turn the eggplant a couple of times and grill until brown and soft.

14. When done, remove the lamb, onions and eggplant and place on a serving platter. Serve hot with lemon wedges.

SQUID NOODLE PASTA

Makes 2 servings

Ingredients

10 ounces squid tubes (calamari), rinsed, cleaned

½ cup mushrooms, sliced

1 clove garlic, sliced

¼ cup chicken stock

½ cup parmesan cheese, grated

Salt to taste

Pepper to taste

1 cup keto friendly tomato sauce

2 tablespoons chopped yellow onion

2 ounces white wine

2 tablespoons olive oil

2 tablespoons fresh basil, chopped

Stevia to taste (optional)

Instructions

1. Place the squid tubes on your cutting board. Slit open one side of each of the tubes so as to lay the tubes flat. Next cut the tube lengthwise so that you get long strips of squid that is now your noodle pasta.

2. Place a skillet over medium heat. Add oil and heat. Add onions and garlic and sauté until translucent.

3. Add wine and mix well. Stir in the tomato sauce. Add stock and let it simmer for a couple of minutes.

4. Add Stevia if desired and mix well.

5. Add mushroom, squid pasta, salt and pepper and stir.

6. Cover and cook until pasta is tender.

7. Add basil and stir. Remove from heat.

8. Serve garnished with cheese.

TUNA FISH SALAD

Makes 2 servings

Ingredients

4 cups mixed greens

½ cup chopped fresh parsley leaves

20 large kalamata olives, pitted

1 avocado, peeled, pitted, diced

2 cans light tuna in water, drained, chopped into chunks

2 large tomatoes, diced

½ cup chopped fresh mint leaves

2 small zucchini, sliced lengthwise

2 green onions, sliced

2 tablespoons extra-virgin olive oil

½ teaspoon Himalayan sea salt or fine sea salt

Instructions

1. Preheat a cast iron grill pan. Place zucchini slices on it and grill on both the sides. Remove the grilled zucchini and place on your cutting board.

2. When cool enough to handle, chop into bite size pieces.

3. Add zucchini into a large bowl. Add rest of the ingredients.

4. Toss well.

5. Serve right away.

2 tablespoons balsamic vinegar

Freshly cracked pepper to taste

BACON AND SHRIMP RISOTTO

Makes 4 servings

Ingredients

4 cups daikon radish or jicama, shredded

4 tablespoons dry white wine

2 cloves garlic, minced

8 ounces shrimp, peeled, deveined, cooked

8 slices pasture raised bacon, chopped

½ cup chicken stock

Salt to taste

Pepper powder to taste

¼ cup chopped fresh parsley

Instructions

1. Squeeze the daikon radish of excess moisture.
2. Place a saucepan over medium heat. Add bacon and cook until crisp.
3. Remove with a slotted spoon and place on a plate. Retain the bacon fat in the pan.
4. Raise the heat to high heat. Add daikon, stock, wine, pepper, salt and garlic and cook until most of the liquid in the pan dries up.
5. Add shrimp and most of the bacon and mix well.
6. Add parsley and stir. Garnish with remaining bacon and serve.

SEAFOOD CHOWDER

Makes 3 servings

Ingredients

1 ½ teaspoons garlic, chopped

1 teaspoon onion powder

¼ cup celery, chopped

1 ½ cups cauliflower, chopped

A handful fresh parsley, chopped

½ tablespoon arrowroot powder

1 teaspoon Old Bay seasoning

1 1/2 ounces without shell shrimp, chopped into small pieces

4 ounce white fish, boneless, chopped into small pieces

2 1/2 ounces clam, minced

½ can clam broth

½ cup heavy cream

Instructions

1. Add celery, cauliflower, chicken broth, onion powder, clam juice, garlic and Old bay seasoning into a soup pot.
2. Place the pot over medium heat. Bring to the boil.
3. Lower heat and cover with a lid. Simmer for 10-12 minutes.
4. Add shrimp, fish, clam and parsley and stir.
5. Simmer for 10 minutes or until tender.
6. Stir in the butter and cream.
7. Mix arrowroot powder with 2 tablespoons water and add into the pot. Stir constantly until thick.
8. Season with salt and pepper.
9. Ladle into soup bowls and serve.

2 tablespoons butter

1 cup chicken broth

Salt to taste

Pepper to taste

SHRIMP CEVICHE STUFFED AVOCADO

Makes 2 (7 shrimp and ½ avocado per serving) servings

Ingredients

14 extra large shrimp, cleaned, deveined

1 large clove garlic, crushed

1 tablespoon fresh cilantro, finely chopped

2 tablespoons white wine vinegar

½ jalapeño, deseeded, finely chopped

1/8 teaspoon ground cumin

2 cups arugula

1 small red onion, sliced

6 grape or cherry tomatoes, halved

½ teaspoon kosher salt

½ tablespoon olive oil

Instructions

1. Place a pot of water over medium heat. When it begins boil add shrimp and simmer until it turns opaque. Drain and place the shrimp immediately in an ice bath.

2. Add all the ingredients except arugula and avocado in a bowl. Mix well and chill for a few hours.

3. To serve: Spread arugula into 2 serving plates. Place an avocado on each. Divide and top with the shrimp mixture.

4. Serve.

1 tablespoon clam juice

Pepper to taste

1 medium Hass avocado, peeled, pitted, halved

CHAPTER THIRTEEN

KETO VEGETARIAN RECIPES

BELL PEPPER BASIL PIZZA

Makes 2 servings

Ingredients

For pizza base:

3 ounces mozzarella cheese

1 tablespoons psyllium husk

1 tablespoon fresh parmesan cheese

½ teaspoon Italian seasoning

¼ teaspoon pepper

¼ cup almond flour

1 tablespoon cream cheese

1 small egg

¼ teaspoon salt

For toppings:

2 ounces shredded cheddar cheese

2 tablespoons keto friendly marinara sauce

Instructions

1. Add mozzarella cheese into a microwave safe bowl and microwave on High for 40-50 seconds or until it melts completely and is workable. Stir every 20 seconds.

2. Add rest of the pizza base ingredients into the bowl and mix well using your hands to form dough.

3. Place on a lined baking sheet.

4. Roll with a rolling pin into a circle.

5. Bake in a preheated oven 400° F for 10 minutes.

6. Spread marinara sauce over the crust. Scatter tomato and bell pepper all over the crust.

7. Sprinkle cheddar cheese and basil on top and bake for 8 to 10 minutes.

8. Cool slightly. Cut into wedges and serve.

A handful fresh basil, chopped

1 small vine tomato, chopped

1 small bell pepper, sliced

KETO NOODLE BOWLS WITH CREAMY CURRY SAUCE

Makes 8 servings

Ingredients

For noodle bowl:

2 packs Kanten noodles

1 head cauliflower, roughly chopped

4 carrots, peeled, julienned

2 red bell peppers, diced

6-8 cups mixed greens

1 cup fresh cilantro, chopped

Hot water, as required

For creamy curry sauce:

½ cup tahini or avocado oil mayonnaise

½ cup water

Instructions

1. The hot water to be used should be more than lukewarm and much lesser than boiling hot, like the one you will be able to drink with ease.

2. Place the noodles in a large bowl. Pour hot water over it and set aside for 5 minutes.

3. Strain the noodles by passing through a fine wire mesh strainer. Transfer into a bowl and set aside to cool. Add carrots, bell pepper, cauliflower and cilantro into the bowl of noodles. Toss well.

4. To make curry sauce: Add all the ingredients for curry sauce into a blender. Blend for 30-40 seconds or until smooth.

5. Pour the curry sauce over the bowl of noodles. Toss well. You can serve immediately or chill and serve later.

6. Leftover noodle bowl can be stored in an airtight container for 2 days.

4 tablespoons avocado oil or MCT oil

4 tablespoons apple cider vinegar

4 teaspoons curry powder

2 teaspoons sea salt

2 teaspoons ground cumin

½ teaspoon ground ginger

3 teaspoons ground coriander

2 teaspoons ground turmeric

1 teaspoon ground black pepper

SESAME TOFU AND EGGPLANT

Makes 8 servings

Ingredients

2 lbs firm tofu

6 tablespoons rice vinegar

4 cloves garlic, minced

4 teaspoons swerve confectioners'

2 tablespoons olive oil

½ cup sesame seeds

2 cups chopped cilantro

8 tablespoons toasted sesame oil

2 teaspoons crushed red pepper flakes

2 whole eggplants (about a lb each")

Salt to taste

Pepper to taste

Instructions

1. Wrap tofu with paper towels and place on a plate. Place something heavy (like a heavy bottom pan or can of fruit) on it to drain excess moisture. Let it remain like this for 30-40 minutes.

2. Add about ½ cup cilantro, 4 tablespoons sesame oil, vinegar, garlic, swerve and red pepper flakes into a bowl and mix well.

3. Peel the eggplants and cut into julienne strips either with a sharp knife or mandolin slicer with a julienne attachment. Add eggplant into it. Toss well and set aside for 5-10 minutes.

4. Place a large skillet or wok over medium heat. Add eggplant with marinade and cook until eggplant is tender.

5. Remove from heat. Add remaining cilantro and stir. Transfer into an oven safe bowl and keep warm.

6. Cut the tofu into 16 equal slices. Place sesame seeds on a plate. Dredge tofu slices in sesame seeds. Press the seeds into the tofu.

7. Wipe the pan clean and place it over medium heat.

8. Add 2 tablespoons of sesame oil and heat.

9. Place a few of the tofu slices and cook until underside is crisp and golden brown. Flip sides and cook the other side until crisp and golden brown.

½ cup tamari or coconut aminos or soy sauce

Remove with a slotted spoon and place on a plate lined with paper towels.

10. Repeat steps 8-9 with the remaining tofu slices.

11. Add all the tofu slices into the pan. Add soy sauce and toss well. Cook until dry. Stir occasionally.

12. Place tofu over noodles and serve.

LOADED CAULIFLOWER

Makes 3 servings

Ingredients

½ lb cauliflower floret's

½ cup grated cheddar cheese

1 tablespoon snipped chives

1/8 teaspoon garlic powder

2 ounces sour cream

1 slice cooked bacon, crumbled

1 ½ tablespoons butter

Salt to taste

Pepper to taste

Instructions

1. Place cauliflower in a microwave safe bowl with a tablespoon of water. Cover and microwave on high for 5-6 minutes or until soft. Drain the liquid from the bowl and let it cool for a few minutes.

2. Transfer into the food processor bowl and process until creamy. Sprinkle salt and pepper and mix well. Transfer into a baking dish.

3. Add most of the chives, and half the cheese and stir.

4. Sprinkle remaining cheese on top.

5. Broil for a few minutes until brown on top. Garnish with bacon and serve.

CHAPTER FOURTEEN

KETO SIDE DISHES

CAULIFLOWER COUSCOUS

Makes 10-12 servings

Ingredients

1 large cauliflower, grated to rice like texture

1 medium green bell pepper, chopped

1 medium red bell pepper, chopped

2 shallots, chopped

1 large tomato, chopped

24 walnuts, chopped into small pieces

4 tablespoons olive oil

Juice of a lemon

1 tablespoon chopped fresh cilantro

Salt to taste

Pepper to taste

Instructions

1. Place a nonstick pan over medium heat. Add oil and heat. Add cauliflower and stir.
2. Lower the heat.
3. Cook until the cauliflower is tender.
4. Add salt and pepper, stir and remove from heat.
5. Transfer into a large bowl.
6. Add rest of the ingredients. Toss well.
7. Taste and adjust the seasonings if necessary.

CAULIFLOWER GARLIC BREADSTICKS

Makes 10 servings

Ingredients

2 heads cauliflower, grated

2 tablespoons butter

5 teaspoons minced garlic

½ teaspoon red pepper flakes (optional)

1 teaspoon Italian seasoning

Kosher salt to taste

2 ½ cups shredded mozzarella cheese, divided

2 large eggs, beaten

1 cup shaved parmesan cheese

1 tablespoon chopped fresh Italian flat-leaf parsley

1 tablespoon chopped fresh basil

Instructions

1. Add cauliflower, Parmesan cheese, 1 cup mozzarella cheese, eggs, garlic, salt, pepper and herbs into a bowl and mix well.

2. Spread on a lined baking sheet. Spread into a rectangle of ¼ inch thickness. Press it well.

3. Bake in a preheated oven 425° F for 10 to 12 minutes.

4. Remove from oven. Sprinkle remaining mozzarella cheese.

5. Bake for another 8-10 minutes or brown on top.

6. Remove from oven. Cut into sticks and serve.

GARLIC GRILLED BROCCOLI

Makes 2 servings

Ingredients

2 cups broccoli florets

¼ teaspoon kosher salt

1 teaspoon garlic powder

¼ teaspoon pepper

¼ teaspoon red pepper flakes or to taste

1 tablespoon olive oil

Instructions

1. Add all the ingredients into a bowl and toss well.
2. Preheat a grill.
3. Place a sheet of aluminum foil on a grill.
4. Grill for 8-10 minutes and cook until crisp as well as tender.

EASY CHEESY ZUCCHINI GRATIN

Makes 4 servings

Ingredients

2 cups zucchini slices

Salt to taste

Pepper to taste

1 tablespoon butter

¼ cup heavy whipping cream

1 small onion, thinly sliced

¾ cup shredded pepper Jack cheese

¼ teaspoon garlic powder

Instructions

1. Place ½ the zucchini slices in a small (6 x6) greased baking dish, overlapping if required.

2. Layer with onion slices. Sprinkle salt and pepper.

3. Next layer with half the cheese.

4. Repeat the 3 layers once more.

5. Add rest of the ingredients into a microwave safe bowl. Microwave on High for a few seconds until melted and smooth. Pour over the layers.

6. Bake in a preheated oven at 350° F for about 30 minutes or until golden brown on top.

BAKED PARMESAN ZUCCHINI ROUNDS

Makes 4-8 servings

Ingredients

4 medium zucchinis, cut into ¼ inch thick, round slices

Garlic salt to taste

1 cup parmesan cheese, freshly grated or more if you like it cheesy

Freshly ground black pepper to taste

Instructions

1. Line a baking sheet with foil. Spray lightly with cooking spray.
2. Place the zucchini slices on the prepared baking sheet, close to each other without overlapping the slices.
3. Season with garlic salt and pepper. Sprinkle Parmesan cheese on the zucchini slices.
4. Bake in a preheated oven at 425° F for about 15-20 minutes or until melted and golden brown.
5. Serve right away.

CREAMY MOCK POTATO MASH

Makes 8 servings

Ingredients

2 large heads cauliflower, chopped into small floret's

4 cloves garlic, minced

1 large onion, chopped

8 tablespoons lard or butter or ghee+ ½ cup extra to top

1 cup cream cheese or sour cream

Salt to taste

Pepper to taste

Instructions

1. Place a pot on medium heat. Pour enough water to cover 2 inches from the bottom of the pot. Place a steaming rack in pot.

2. Place the cauliflower florets in a heatproof bowl. Place the bowl on the rack. Cover and steam the cauliflower for 10 minutes or until tender. Be careful not to overcook it.

3. Remove cauliflower from the pot and set aside.

4. Place a skillet over medium heat. Add 2 tablespoons butter or ghee and melt. Add onions and garlic and sauté until the onions are translucent.

5. Add remaining butter and stir. Turn off the heat. Transfer into a blender. Add cauliflower and blend until smooth.

6. Add cream cheese and pulse for 3-4 seconds or until well combined.

7. Transfer into a bowl. Add salt and pepper to taste.

8. Top with extra butter and serve.

CHINESE VEGETABLE STIR-FRY

Makes 8 servings

Ingredients

2/3 cup soy sauce or coconut aminos or tamari

4 tablespoons dry sherry or Chinese rice wine

4 teaspoons erythritol or to taste

½ teaspoon red pepper flakes

4 tablespoons vegetable oil

14 ounces shiitake mushrooms, stems removed, thinly sliced

6 cloves garlic, finely chopped

2 tablespoons ginger, grated

6 tablespoons water

2 teaspoons sesame oil

2 tablespoons arrowroot starch

½ teaspoon dry mustard

Instructions

1. Add soy sauce, dry sherry, erythritol, red pepper flakes, water, sesame oil, cornstarch and mustard into a bowl and stir until well combined.

2. Place a large nonstick skillet over medium heat. Pour enough water to cover 1 inch from the bottom of the pan. When it begins to boil, add broccoli and cook for 2-3 minutes, until broccoli is crisp as well as tender.

3. Drain and rinse under cold running water. Drain and set aside.

4. Clean the pan and place over high heat. Add vegetable oil and heat.

5. Add red bell peppers and mushrooms and sauté for a few minutes until tender.

6. Stir in the garlic, ginger and white and light green part of the scallions. Stir constantly until aromatic.

7. Add broccoli into the pan and heat thoroughly. Add the sauce mixture and toss well. Stir frequently until the sauce is well coated over the vegetables.

8. Garnish with the dark green part of scallions and serve over cauliflower rice.

2 lbs broccoli, cut into 1 inch florets

2 red bell peppers, thinly sliced

6 scallions, thinly sliced, keep the white and light green parts together and dark green part separately

GINGER AND GARLIC BOK CHOY STIR-FRY

Makes 4 servings

Ingredients

10 bunches Bok Choy, cut the ends, chopped into 1 inch pieces

2 teaspoons grated fresh ginger

4 cloves garlic, minced

2 tablespoons coconut oil

Salt to taste

Instructions

1. Place a wok over medium heat. Add oil and heat. Add boy Choy and sauté until it wilts.

2. Add ginger, garlic and salt. Sauté for a couple of minutes and remove from heat.

3. Serve hot.

ROASTED CAULIFLOWER STEAKS

Makes 8 servings

Ingredients

2 tablespoons lemon juice

2 heads cauliflower, stems removed, rinsed

4 cloves garlic, crushed

¼ cup fresh parsley

Instructions

1. Stir lemon juice and garlic in a bowl and set it aside for a while for the flavors to blend in.

2. Hold the cauliflower on your cutting board and start slicing it into ¾ inch thick slices (do not separate florets)

3. Place the cauliflower slices on a lined baking sheet. Brush the slices with lemon juice mixture and place the garlic on the baking sheet.

4. Roast in a preheated oven at 375° F until golden brown.

5. Garnish with parsley and serve.

CHAPTER FIFTEEN

KETO DESERTS

NUTTY BLACKBERRY FAT BOMBS

Makes 6 servings

Ingredients

1 ounce macadamia nuts, crushed

½ cup blackberry

½ cup coconut oil

¼ teaspoon vanilla extract

¼ teaspoon lemon juice

2 ounces Neufchatel cheese (cream cheese)

1 ½ tablespoons mascarpone cheese

½ cup coconut butter

Stevia to taste (optional)

Instructions

1. Crush the macadamia nuts with a rolling pin. Add the crushed nuts into a small baking dish. Press it well into the bottom of the dish.

2. Let the oven preheat to 325°F.

3. Place the baking dish in the oven. Bake for 5-8 minutes or until golden brown in color. Remove from the oven and set aside to cool.

4. Layer the crust with cream cheese.

5. Add blackberries, coconut oil, mascarpone cheese, coconut butter, lemon juice, vanilla extract and Stevia into a bowl and mix until well combined.

6. Spread this over the cream cheese layer.

7. Place the dish in the freezer for about 30 minutes. Remove from the freezer after 30 minutes and place in the refrigerator. Chill for a few hours.

8. Cut into slices and serve.

KETO VANILLA POUND CAKE

Makes 6 servings

Ingredients

2 cups almond flour

½ cup butter

1 cup erythritol

2 teaspoons baking powder

1 teaspoon vanilla extract

1 cup sour cream

2 oz. cream cheese

4 large eggs

Instructions

1. Preheat the oven to 350 degrees F.
2. Grease a Bundt pan with some butte and set aside.
3. IN a large bowl, combine almond flour with some baking powder and mix well using a spoon.
4. Now, cut the butter into small squares and set aside in a bowl. Add some cream cheese to it.
5. Melt the butter and cream cheese by microwaving it for 30 seconds. Make sure that you don't burn the cheese. Now stir all the wet ingredients properly using a spoon.
6. To this, add some vanilla extract, erythritol, and sour cream to the cream cheese and butter mixture. Stir well using a spoon.
7. Now pour the wet ingredients into the dry ingredients and stir again.
8. Gently crack open the eggs and add it to the batter and mix until there are no lumps.
9. Pour the batter into the greased pan and place it in the oven.
10. Bake it for 50 minutes. You can use a toothpick to check the doneness of the cake.

1. Allow the cake to rest for about 2 hours or overnight for best results. Removing it too soon can make it crumble.

MOCHA AND COCONUT MUG CAKE

Makes 2 servings

Ingredients

2 large eggs, at room temperature

4 tablespoons almond flour

14 drops Stevia

4 tablespoons butter, at room temperature

2 tablespoons erythritol

1 teaspoon baking powder

2 tablespoons cocoa powder, unsweetened

4 teaspoons coconut flour

2 tablespoons unsweetened shredded coconut + extra to serve

1 teaspoon instant coffee

2 tablespoons coconut milk, at room temperature

Instructions

1. Add all the ingredients into a bowl and mix well.
2. Divide equally and pour into 2 mugs.
3. Microwave on high for 70 seconds.
4. Cool for a while. Run a knife around the edges of the mug. Invert on to a plate.
5. Garnish with shredded coconut and serve.

VEGAN COCONUT MACAROONS

Makes 24 yields servings

Ingredients

½ cup almond flour

2 1/2 cups unsweetened desiccated coconut

1 teaspoon vanilla extract

½ cup monk fruit sweetener

½ cup aquafaba

½ teaspoon almond extract

A pinch of salt

½ cup vegan dark chocolate

Instructions

1. Preheat the oven to 350 degrees F.
2. Linea baking dish some parchment paper or grease it with some butter.
3. Heat a small pan on low flame. Add the coconut flakes and roast them lightly for about 3-4 minutes while stirring them often. Make sure you don't forget to stir the coconut aminos while roasting them or else they may turn brown.
4. Remove the coconut flakes in a bowl. To this, add some almond flour, salt and mix well using a spoon. Next, add almond extract, vanilla extract and monk fruit sweetener and mix again using your hands.
5. Now you can make round cookie scoops and add them on the baking sheet.
6. Place the baking sheet inside the oven and bake for about 20 minutes.
7. Melt ½ cup of vegan dark chocolate in the microwave or on the double boiler. Once the cookies are completely done and cooled off, dip each of these cookies into the chocolate dip and place them on a large plate on by one.
8. Refrigerate these cookies for about 30 minutes and serve it alongside your favourite non-dairy milk.

MOCHA AND COCONUT MUG CAKE

Makes 2 servings

Ingredients

2 large eggs, at room temperature

4 tablespoons almond flour

14 drops Stevia

4 tablespoons butter, at room temperature

2 tablespoons erythritol

1 teaspoon baking powder

2 tablespoons cocoa powder, unsweetened

4 teaspoons coconut flour

2 tablespoons unsweetened shredded coconut + extra to serve

1 teaspoon instant coffee

2 tablespoons coconut milk, at room temperature

Instructions

1. Add all the ingredients into a bowl and mix well.
2. Divide equally and pour into 2 mugs.
3. Microwave on high for 70 seconds.
4. Cool for a while. Run a knife around the edges of the mug. Invert on to a plate.
5. Garnish with shredded coconut and serve.

VEGAN COCONUT MACAROONS

Makes 24 yields servings

Ingredients

½ cup almond flour

2 1/2 cups unsweetened desiccated coconut

1 teaspoon vanilla extract

½ cup monk fruit sweetener

½ cup aquafaba

½ teaspoon almond extract

A pinch of salt

½ cup vegan dark chocolate

Instructions

1. Preheat the oven to 350 degrees F.

2. Linea baking dish some parchment paper or grease it with some butter.

3. Heat a small pan on low flame. Add the coconut flakes and roast them lightly for about 3-4 minutes while stirring them often. Make sure you don't forget to stir the coconut aminos while roasting them or else they may turn brown.

4. Remove the coconut flakes in a bowl. To this, add some almond flour, salt and mix well using a spoon. Next, add almond extract, vanilla extract and monk fruit sweetener and mix again using your hands.

5. Now you can make round cookie scoops and add them on the baking sheet.

6. Place the baking sheet inside the oven and bake for about 20 minutes.

7. Melt ½ cup of vegan dark chocolate in the microwave or on the double boiler. Once the cookies are completely done and cooled off, dip each of these cookies into the chocolate dip and place them on a large plate on by one.

8. Refrigerate these cookies for about 30 minutes and serve it alongside your favourite non-dairy milk.

EASY ORANGE CAKE BALLS

Makes 15 balls servings

Ingredients

2/3 cup almond butter

1/3 cup coconut flour + a little bit more for rolling

Zest of 2 oranges

¼ cup orange juice

35 drops of Stevia

½ teaspoon vanilla

1/8 teaspoon salt

Instructions

1. Wash the oranges thoroughly under some running water and pat them dry using paper towels. Now using a grater, zest them. Set aside.

2. In a bowl, add some coconut flour, salt, orange zest and mix well.

3. Now slowly pour the orange juice in the bowl while stirring it continually. Make sure you mix al the ingredients well using a spoon and that there are no lumps. It may take a while to form a smooth mixture, so just be patient with it.

4. Melt some butter in a microwave and add it to the bowl. Mix again.

5. If you feel that the batter is a little too dry, try adding some avocado oil, whereas if you feel it's too wet, and feel free to add some coconut flour to it.

6. Now using your hands roll out about 15 balls by placing a scoop of the mixture n between your palms and squeezing them into shape and smoothen them out.

7. Spread some coconut flour on a flat dish. Lightly roll out each of these cake balls in the coconut flour and place them on a plate.

8. Place the plate inside the refrigerator for about 20 minutes to chill.

9. Serve.

RASPBERRY CHEESECAKE IN CHOCOLATE

Makes 8 servings

Ingredients

4 1/2 ounces mascarpone cheese or full fat cream cheese or creamed coconut milk

½ teaspoon vanilla extract or ¼ teaspoon vanilla bean powder

¼ cup almond flour

10 drops Stevia (optional)

½ cup frozen raspberries

1 tablespoons erythritol or swerve, powdered

2 tablespoons coconut flour

For coating:

3/4 ounce cacao butter or extra virgin coconut oil

1 1/2 ounces 90% dark chocolate

Instructions

1. Add mascarpone cheese, raspberries and erythritol into the food processor bowl. Process until smooth.

2. Add almond flour and coconut flour and process until well combined.

3. Spoon into ice tray (about 2 tablespoons in each ice mold). Freeze for an hour.

4. For coating: Add coconut oil and dark chocolate into a heatproof bowl. Place the bowl in a double boiler. Stir occasionally until the mixture melted.

5. Remove the bowl from the double boiler.

6. Line a tray with parchment paper.

7. Remove the cheesecake from the ice tray and dip into the chocolate mixture.

8. Place on the prepared tray. Freeze until set. Transfer into an airtight container.

9. Store in the freezer until use.

KETO CARROT CAKE WITH CREAM CHEESE FROSTING

Makes 3-4 servings

Ingredients

For the cake

2 tablespoons almond flour

1 tablespoon psyllium husk

1 tablespoon erythritol

1 large egg

½ teaspoon vanilla extract

1 small carrot, finely grated

1/8 teaspoon of salt

1 teaspoon ground cinnamon

¼ teaspoon ground ginger

¼ teaspoon ground cloves

1 tablespoon melted butter

For the frosting

Instructions

1. In a large bowl, gently crack open the egg and whisk them using a fork. You can also beat it with a hand blender.

2. To this bowl, add all the remaining ingredients for the cake and mix well using your hands, spoon or a blender. Regardless of which method you chose, just ensure that everything is combined well and that there are no lumps.

3. You simply add this batter to a microwave bowl and microwave it for about 90 seconds. Take out the cake from the bowl and allow it to cool off for about 15-20 minutes. Once done, slice the cake into 2 layers.

4. In a bowl, add some erythritol, vanilla extract and cream cheese and mix it well. You can use a hand blender and whip all the ingredients together on high speed until you get a nice and creamy texture. Next, add the whipping cream and mix once again for about 4 minutes. Set aside.

5. Place one layer of cake on a plate and add a scoop of the cream cheese frosting on it. Using a butter knife or a spoon spread the frosting all over on top of the cake.

¼ cup cream cheese

1 tablespoon whipping cream

½ tablespoon vanilla extract

½ tablespoon erythritol

6. Now place the second layer of the cake on top and add some more frosting on it. Spread it evenly using the same method.

7. Now empty the remaining frosting on top and coat the entire cake with it.

8. Chill it in the refrigerator for about 30 minutes before serving.

KETO AVOCADO BROWNIES

Makes 2 squares servings

Ingredients

2 large avocados

½ teaspoon vanilla

4 tablespoons cocoa powder

1 teaspoon Stevia

3 tablespoons organic coconut oil

2 large eggs

½ cup keto friendly chocolate chips

Dry ingredients

¼ cup almond flour

¼ teaspoon salt

1 teaspoon baking powder

¼ teaspoon baking soda

Instructions

1. Preheat the oven to 370 degrees F.
2. Wash the avocados properly under some running water and peel them. Now roughly cut them into slices using a sharp kitchen knife and add them to food processor. Process the avocado until they are smooth. Make sure there are no lumps.
3. IN the meanwhile, melt the chocolate in a double boiler or inside the microwave.
4. Now combine the chocolate and avocado mixture and stir well using a large spoon.
5. One by one, start adding all the other ingredients such as vanilla, Stevia powder, cocoa powder, 2 eggs, coconut oil and mix again. For better results, crack the eggs into a small bowl and whisk them properly using a fork before adding them to the avocado and chocolate mixture.
6. In a separate bowl, add the dry ingredients and mix them well. Slowly add them to the chocolate mixture and keep stirring while you are at it. Whisk the mixture in the food processor until it blends well.//
1. Line a baking tray with some parchment paper and pour the batter into it.

1 tablespoon xylitol

7. Place the tray inside the oven and bake for 35 minutes. You can use a toothpick to check its doneness.

8. Allow it to cool off for about 15 minutes, slice it up and serve.

ALMOND JOY CHIA PUDDING

Makes 4 servings

Ingredients

2 cups almond milk, unsweetened

½ cup coconut flakes, separated

¼ cup cocoa powder

¼ cup erythritol

1 teaspoon vanilla extract

1/3 cup chia seeds

10-12 almonds

¼ cup dark chocolate chips, sugar-free

Instructions

1. Heat a small pan on medium flame. Add the almonds to it and roast them for about 4-5 minutes until they are nice and brown and crunchy. Allow them to cool off for about 5 minutes and then crush them using a rolling pin. Set aside.

2. IN a bowl, add some almond milk, cocoa powder, erythritol, coconut flakes and vanilla extract and whisk all the ingredients using a hand blender. You can also add the same mixture to a food processor and mix them vigorously until they form a smooth paste.

3. Add some chia seeds and whisk again.

4. Now transfer the pudding into 4 separate bowls or cups and refrigerate it for 2 hours.

5. Top the pudding with some roasted and crushed almonds, some chocolate chips and coconut flakes and serve.

AVOCADO POPSICLE WITH LIME AND COCONUT

Makes 6 servings

Ingredients

2 large avocados

1 1/2 cups almond milk

¼ cup erythritol

2 tablespoons lime juice

Instructions

1. Wash the avocados properly and pat them dry using paper towels. Now slice them up and pit them.

2. Add the avocados to the blender along with almond milk, erythritol and lime juice and cover with a lid. You can try scraping the insides of the blender to incorporate the splattered ingredients.

3. Blend the mixture into a smooth and creamy consistency. Make sure there are no lumps.

4. Place 6 Popsicle mold on the kitchen top.

5. Now evenly pour the batter into each of the molds. It's possible that since the blended liquid is thick, you may find it easier to add it using a spoon rather than pouring it directly into the molds. Go with what makes you feel comfortable.

6. Gently tap on the sides of the molds to remove all the air bubbles while being able to settle the mixture.

7. Insert Popsicle sticks right in the center of the molds and place them inside the freezer for several hours. This could take about 10-12 hours.

8. When you are all set to eat them, run all the molds under some running water for a brief while to help release the popsicles.

9. Gently pull out the stick and enjoy your popsicles.

CHOCOLATE COCONUT KETO ICE CREAM

Makes 10 yields servings

Ingredients

1 ripe avocado

13 oz. coconut cream, frozen in cubes

3 tablespoons of cocoa powder

A pinch of salt

20 drops of Stevia

Instructions

1. Wash the avocados properly and pat them dry using paper towels. Now slice them up and pit them.

2. Add the avocados to a blender along with some coconut cream, cocoa powder, salt, and Stevia drops. Blend all the ingredients well until the mixture turns smooth and creamy. You may need to scrape the insides of the blender and re-blend two or three times. If you aren't able to get a smooth consistency, you can add about one or two tablespoons of water slowly until it appears silky and rich.

3. Make sure there are no lumps.

4. Refrigerate the ice cream for about 3-4 hours and serve.

PEANUT BUTTER POPSICLES

Makes 6 servings

Ingredients

1 can (13 1/2 ounces) coconut milk

½ teaspoon toffee flavored liquid Stevia

¼ cup peanut butter, unsweetened

Instructions

1. Add all the ingredients into a blender and blend until smooth.

2. Pour into Popsicle molds. Insert sticks. Freeze until set.

LOW-CARB VANILLA BEAN ICE CREAM

Makes 6-7 servings

Ingredients

4 large eggs

4 or 5 egg yolks

1 tablespoon lemon juice

7 tablespoons ghee, melted

5 tablespoons cacao butter, melted

5 tablespoons coconut oil, melted

3 tablespoons Stevia

2 tablespoons water

2 teaspoons vanilla powder

2 tablespoons chocolate chips

Instructions

1. Crack the eggs into a blender and blend them. Now add the egg yolks and blend once again.

2. One by one add all the remaining ingredients from the list and whisk on high power for about 2 minutes until you get a rich and creamy paste.

3. You can feel free to add some more sweetener if required.

4. Now pour the batter slowly into an ice-cream maker and churn it for about 15-20 minutes. If you don't have an ice cream maker, you can simply keep stirring it for about 10-15 minutes.

5. Refrigerate for 4-5 hours, with some chocolate chips and serve.

CONCLUSION

I wanted to thank you once again for choosing this book.

This book will show my readers a realistic picture of the keto journey that they are about to take. My intention is not to discourage anyone from taking up the ketogenic diet, but when you are aware of what it's like to follow the diet, you will find it much easier to stick to it. And that's exactly what I want all of you to do.

Stick to the ketogenic diet; even embrace it as a part of your lifestyle to get long-term results.

To make the diet easy for you, I have listed a wide range of keto friendly recipes that range from breakfast, snack, meals and desserts etc. One thing for sure, you will not be short of choices when it comes to choosing the right recipe as long as you refer to the book.

Lastly, if you liked this book, don't forget to leave a positive review and share it with your friends and family.

Thank you once again and good luck in your ketogenic journey.

www.ingramcontent.com/pod-product-compliance
Lightning Source LLC
Chambersburg PA
CBHW051350070526
44584CB00025B/3712